Sin
in the
HOUSE

Ten Crucial Church Problems
with Cleansing Solutions

By
George O. McCalep, Ph.D.

Sin
in the
HOUSE

Ten Crucial Church Problems with Cleansing Solutions

Sin in the House
Copyright © 1999 by Orman Press, Inc.
Lithonia, GA

ISBN: 1-891773-06-2

Printed in the United States of America

Table *of* Contents

Foreword

Dr. George O. McCalep has a special mantle upon him in the area of church growth. While I hesitate to use the word "expert" to describe Dr. McCalep's knowledge and experience concerning church growth, I can say without hesitation that God has placed a special anointing upon him in the ministry of church growth.

Greenforest Community Baptist Church, under Dr. McCalep's leadership, serves as a living testimony to the mantle that God has so graciously bestowed upon him.

In *Sin in the House*, Dr. McCalep details ten crucial church growth problems that are plaguing churches today. Dr. McCalep confronts and exposes the sins of carnality, cruelty and complacency in the church, citing them as partial reasons for the absence of church growth in many contemporary churches. He presents a biblical definition of carnality, not relegating that definition solely to sexual immorality, as is often done.

While the definition of carnality certainly does not exclude sexual sins, Dr. McCalep uses a biblical foundation to expand that definition to focus on forms of carnality that are generally deemed as more acceptable behavior, even within the church. Because such behaviors are considered acceptable, we often ignore the subtle carnality that can and will stifle the growth of any church.

Reading this book will convict as well as challenge our philosophy as it pertains to church growth and the reasons for the lack of it in so many churches.

Dr. McCalep challenges us to change the way we think about church growth. He exposes and explains the seldom seen, yet powerful impediments to Christian ministry.

I believe that God has delivered a profound message for the body of Christ through this book.

If we as pastors, church leaders, and believers in Jesus Christ are seriously committed to growth of the church — both numerically and spiritually—we will make sure that *Sin in the House* is cataloged in our hearts and minds, and that it has a permanent space in our libraries.

> And the Lord added to the church daily
> such as should be saved. (Acts 2:47)

Bishop Victor T. Curry
Senior Pastor/Teacher
New Birth Baptist Church
Miami, Florida

INTRODUCTION

Ten Crucial Church Growth Problems

...the primary reason churches don't grow is because of the carnality within the body of Christ.

Churches across this country excuse their lack of growth to minimal resources, location, or other various circumstances and situations. This book is based on the premise that the primary reason churches don't grow is because of the carnality within the body of Christ. The term carnality does not refer exclusively to the sins of lust, as some often think sexual immorality is not a topic of discussion in this book. Carnality refers to any thinking or behavior that is contrary to the will of God based on our best interpretation of scripture. For example, secular thinking is definitely carnal. The scriptures tell us clearly to

"lean not unto thine own understanding." (Proverb. 3:5)

...one of the main problems of the church is that she has adopted many of the procedures and practices of society that are not scripturally or biblically based.

This book is not intended to present any new profound theological interpretation of scripture. Rather, as previously stated, it is scripturally based on an interpretation that the great majority of Christians will probably agree with. The question or challenge is: If we agree that this is what God is saying, then why don't we do it? It is intended that nothing in this book will be presented that is not biblically based. The idea is to bring the church into conformity with scripture in every aspect of its existence.

As will be discussed in the following chapters, one of the main problems of the church is that she has adopted many of the procedures and practices of society that are not scripturally or biblically based. This is sin. There is sin in the house of God among the people of God. If God's church is to grow, we must clean the house.

I thank God for blessing me with ignorance relative to the cruelty of God's people when I first began my pastorate. At that time I was ignorant and naive to the fact that church people can be cruel. If I had been aware that God's people could be so cruel I seriously doubt whether I would have survived. I simply did not know what was troubling and causing some of the members to act so cruelly, especially when the church began to grow.

Church growth can ignite cruel behavior in church members. This whole matter of cruelty and sin in the house has been historically treated like a "sacred cow." It has not been debunked. No one has looked behind the scenes or behind the curtain. In other words, it is not to be talked about or exposed openly. It has been ignored, walked around, swept under the carpet, and only talked about behind closed doors. However, the purpose of this book is to reveal it, to expose it, to illustrate it, to dramatize it, and to correct it by conforming to scripture. The ultimate goal is to eradicate it (sin), thereby releasing the power of God for kingdom building and church growth.

Sin in the House is not intended to stand in judgment of the church's salvation. Nor is it intended to bring into question the salvation of the people of God. It is not the purpose of this book to question or challenge the doctrine of eternal security. I believe in the doctrine of eternal security. You only have to be saved once, not over and over again. However, one of the crucial church problems to be discussed in this book is called "stuck on salvation."

...salvation does not guarantee discipleship

The problem of the church is not one of salvation but rather behaving as though salvation, getting saved, or helping others become saved is the end of the church's responsibility. This is not true according to scripture. For example, salvation does not guarantee discipleship. Therefore, it is sin to be stuck on salvation. There is sin in the house.

The Church – A Backsliding Heifer

The church is in a backslidden posture.

The problem is not salvation. The problem is one commonly referred to as backsliding. The church is in a backslidden posture. Backsliding refers to being stubborn, unwilling to move, unwilling to change. In Hosea 4:16, God refers to the house of Israel as a backsliding heifer. The New Testament church is the New Israel, and the position is the same. When I was growing up in the state of Alabama, to call someone a heifer was considered very negative. It could be compared to calling a woman a bitch today. Though a bitch is actually a female dog, and a heifer is a young female calf, to call a woman a bitch is obscene. I believe God set the tone of His displeasure for our backsliding by calling us (the church) a backsliding heifer.

To get the picture as well as to feel the drama of this scriptural rebuke, we must try to understand the nature of a backsliding heifer. As a youngster in Alabama, I literally experienced the difficulty of dealing with a backsliding heifer. The picture is that of trying to lead a young female calf (heifer) into the back of a pickup truck. This was before the day of hydraulic or automatic lifts. The task was to get the stubborn heifer to walk up an inclined plank at the back of the truck. A few boys would be in the front of the heifer pulling her while others would get behind her and push. It was a difficult task. With much effort and time, we would get the heifer to take a few steps, but just as she nearly reached the top of the incline, she would lock her front legs and start sliding backwards. So the pulling and pushing and encouraging would have to start all over again. God is saying that this is a picture of the church. God calls the church a backsliding heifer. The church has locked her legs on change. The church is sliding backwards. Though many churches begin new ministries with good intentions, they simply do not or cannot follow through due to their inability to change.

Many churches are still doing church the same as they did forty plus years ago.

Mainline churches are declining in membership. Society has an increasing disrespect for the church and her value. Many churches are dying because they embrace the seven last words of the dying church, "We've never done it that way before." Change is essential for growth. I am not referring to change or compromise of scripture. The word of God never changes. It is the same today as it was yesterday. The word of God is eternal. The Gospel message never changes. The message of the old rugged cross never changes. The cross is rugged, it cannot be polished or glittered. It cannot be romanticized. The message of the incarnate God who died a substitutionary death for the forgiveness of the sin of the world should not be, and cannot be changed. However, the method and the various approaches to presenting the messages must change. Many churches are still doing church the same way they did forty plus years ago. Forty years ago, our music was presented to the world on breakable 78 rpm records. The music world has progressed from 78 rpm to 45 rpm, to 33$\frac{1}{3}$ rpm, to 8-track, cassette, and now compact discs. The sad commentary is that many churches are still spinning 78's, while existing in a CD era.

Methodology changes are absolutely necessary to reach new generations of people. Studies show that a lower and lower percentage of younger generations actually go to church, or even value church at all. It is a sin for the church to be so stubborn that it is not willing to change for the express purpose of reaching more people for the kingdom of God. Failure to change because we like church a certain way is sin. There is sin in the house. This book will attempt to dramatize the problems of church that prohibit growth. The church needs to see herself in her carnality and correct herself in obedience to scripture. For example, consider how many church members stroll down the aisle and look at a first-time visitor who may be sitting in their customary every Sunday seat or pew. Many members will stop and stare at the visitor as if to say, "Who are you and why are you in my seat?" Some will even nudge the visitor to move over. The visitor may not leave at that time, but they get the message. The message is "You are in my seat." Even if the visitor does not move then, they have gotten the message and probably will not come

Failure to change because we like church a certain way is sin.

back. The church is guilty of sin. That behavior was an act of the flesh, and it displeases God. God says we are His ambassadors (2 Corinthians 5:20). We are fellow laborers with Him. How can we be ambassadors and fellow laborers if we do not give up our seat gladly to make a sinner feel welcome in the house of God?

Noteworthy, Jesus begins (John 2:14-16) and ends His ministry (Mark 11:15 and Luke 19:45) by cleaning house. We can never be sure of the chronology of events recorded in the gospels. In the fourth gospel according to the beloved disciple, John, an event of house cleaning by Jesus took place at the beginning of His earthly ministry, right after Jesus had brought forth His first miracle by turning water to wine in Galilee. Recorded in all the synoptic gospels, Jesus ends His earthly ministry by cleaning God's house. It was the Monday after Palm Sunday: the day after He had proclaimed His messiahship by His triumphant ride into Jerusalem on a donkey (colt), ever so meek, yet ever so regal and royal.

In verse 11 of Mark's version, Jesus finished His Palm Sunday by examining the temple in Jerusalem. He evidently concluded that it was dirty because the next morning He returned with a display of anger and cleaned it. Jesus said, "My house shall be called of all nations the house of prayer: but ye have made it a den of thieves." Notice, Jesus said, "My house." The church is God's house, but we have defiled it by trying to make it our house. It is a sin to consider God's house "our" house. We can own the vision of the house, but we cannot own the house. There is sin in the house. Jesus knew this was the

It is a sin to consider God's house our house.

house for which He was soon to give His life. Jesus even cast out some people in the house. Scripture records that He cast out: (1) those who secularized and commercialized His house; (2) those who desecrated His house; (3) those who affected the atmosphere of prayer. Remember, praise is a part of prayer; (4) those who shut out other people. He said my house is for all nations; and (5) those who changed the purpose of the temple. Oh, how guilty we are! We have strayed from the five-fold biblical purposes of the church: (1) worship; (2) fellowship; (3) discipleship; (4) evangelism; and (5) service. We have strayed from Jesus' main agenda which is to seek and save.

Oh, how we have messed up God's house! If He would come today to once again examine and clean house, would you and your church be cast out? Jesus is not coming again to clean house. He expects us to clean house. He is coming again to claim a prepared house. How long will He tarry before He comes? We know not the time nor the hour. But we must work (clean) while it is day, for the night cometh when no man can work (Matthew 25;13).

There is sin in the house! We must clean house. We are the house. The scripture tells us that our bodies are the temple of the Holy Spirit (1 Corinthians 6:19). We, the baptized believers, make up the body of Christ, which is the house of God. The house is dirty. God chooses not to grow dirty houses. We have grieved the Holy Spirit by forcing

God chooses not to grow dirty houses. We have grieved the Holy Spirit by forcing Him to live in a dirty house.

Him to live in a dirty house. It is time to clean the house. *Sin in the House* will present and explore the use of scripture narrative along with real church and life illustrations to show Ten Crucial Church Problems. These are problems that are sinful in nature and prohibit church growth.

This book presents a word from God for reproof and correction. In addition, each chapter contains suggested house cleaning solutions. House cleaning solutions are intended to be corrective suggestions that will help or eliminate the crucial problems addressed in the chapter. It is not suggested that all churches are guilty of all the crucial church problems presented. But most churches are guilty of at least some of them. Also, after each chapter, there is a review section designed to help recapture the essentials necessary to deal with the problem. Scripture tells us that a little leaven "leaveneth the whole lump" (1 Corinthians 5:6). Sin left uncorrected can cause many believers and churches to fail in their calling and responsibilities to God.

> Purge out therefore the old leaven, that ye may be a new lump, as ye are unleavened. For even Christ our passover is sacrificed for us Therefore let us keep the feast, not with old leaven, neither with the leaven of malice and wickedness; but with the unleavened bread of sincerity and truth. (1 Corinthians. 5:7-8)

God's people of the Old Testament were required not to sweep the leaven under the carpet. Rather, they were to sweep all the leaven out of the house in preparation for the Passover (Exodus. 12:15).

Leaven symbolizes the power of sin when left in the house. The meal is a figure of speech for Christ. As God's people of the Old Testament were required to remove all leaven from the celebration of the Passover, the church today is expected to clean God's house by removing all contamination.

It is my prayer that churches and individual Christians will make a deliberate decision to come into obedience with the word of God and release the growth potential of the kingdom of God. There is sin in the house, but obedience to God's word can eradicate sin. We are cleansed by the word of God (John 15:3). Read this book. If applicable, see yourself and your church. Be obedient and let God's word clean.

CHAPTER ONE

Cursed Giving

One of the problems that has stifled church growth is cursed giving. The Bible speaks considerably about how we should give, and the rewards and consequences of giving as God says to give. In the familiar tithing scriptures (Malachi 3:8-10) God declares:

> Will a man rob God? Yet ye have robbed me. But ye say, Wherein have we robbed thee? In tithes and offerings. Ye are cursed with a curse: for ye have robbed me, even this whole nation. Bring ye all the tithes into the storehouse, that there may be meat in mine house, and prove me now herewith, saith the LORD of hosts, if I will not open you the windows of heaven, and pour you out a blessing, that there shall not be room enough to receive it.

Typically, when we teach that scripture we skip verse nine that states, "Ye are cursed with a curse: for ye have robbed me, even this whole nation." Ignoring verse nine is another example of sweeping the sin of the church under the carpet. God tells us that we are blessed if we tithe, and we are cursed if we don't. The whole church is cursed. Therefore, the community is cursed, and the nation is cursed.

If you are not a tither, you are out of the will of God.

We hear much about welfare use, welfare reform, and welfare abuse. However, we hear little about how God's people have abused the church by withholding their tithe. We need to consider an "Act of Church Reform" to conform to what the Bible tells us about tithing. If all the church members in any given city in America were tithers we would not need welfare. Due to the disobedience of the church, the nation is under a curse. God said,

Bring me all the tithes into the storehouse (the church), so that there may be meat in mine house. (Malachi 3:10)

God's house has no meat because there is sin in the house. In most churches the percentages of tithers range from 10 to 20 percent of the total congregation. That leaves approximately 80 percent of the total congregation out of the will of God. Make no mistake about this fact, if you are not a tither, you are out of the will of God. The church is out of the will of God.

HOW IS THIS PROBLEM SEEN IN THE CHURCH?

The church that I pastor, the Greenforest Community Baptist Church, has grown quite proud of its continuously increasing contributions from tithes and offerings. In the past twenty years, the operating budget has increased from $30,000 to $3,500,000. However, there are 3,000 family units that are contributors. For budgeting administration we categorize the membership into family units (a single adult represents one unit, and a family with ten children represents only one unit).

According to the latest demographic statistics received from the county data bank, the average income in the county in which our church is located is $30,000 per year. If you multiply $30,000 by 3,000 contributing units, the purchasing power of the congregation is $90 million. If all the contributing family units were tithing 10%, as thus saith the Lord, the church income would at least be 10% of $90 million which is $9 million. Remember, I said the actual income is only $3.5 million. The difference between what should be and what actually has been received is $5.5 million. I have concluded, therefore, that I preach to $5.5 million worth of sin each Sunday. There is sin in the house.

Using that formula, I pastor at least $5.5 million of sin. There is sin in the house. I asked a few of my neighboring pastors to use the same formula and calculate how much sin they pastor. Just within the immediate neighborhood we concluded that we preach to over $50 million worth of sin each Sunday. There is sin in the house. Using the same formula for the church of your affiliation, how much sin is in the house?

Will a man rob God? Yes. We rob God at least every Sunday morning. At eleven o'clock on Sunday morning the "Great God Robbery" takes place. A bigger robbery cannot be found among the criminal archives of the world. Christians, the great percentage of those who pro-

...the great percentage of those who profess to His saving power are found in the posture of robbing the very one they claim to love.

fess to His saving power are found in the posture of robbing the very one they claim to love.

The consequences:

> "Ye are cursed with a curse: for ye have robbed me, even this whole nation." (Malachi 3:9).

However, God has provided a provision for us to be delivered from this curse. God says, Bring ye all the tithes into the storehouse, that there may be meat in mine house, and prove me now herewith, saith the Lord of hosts, if I will not open you the windows of heaven, and pour you out a blessing, that there shall not be room enough to receive it. God promises that if the church will be obedient to his commandment it will be blessed:

> "And all nations shall call you blessed: for ye shall be a delightsome land, saith the Lord of hosts." (Malachi 3:12)

HOUSE CLEANING SOLUTIONS

SOLUTION ONE: *Stop selling for profit and commercializing in the church.*

For years churches have been selling for profit and commercializing in the house. Such fundraising is simply not scriptural. Selling chicken dinners to do ministry is not biblical. Nowhere in the Bible does it suggest that we should raise money by selling or commercializing in the church. We have added to the curse by playing bingo (a form of gaming/gambling), selling dinner tickets, raffles, and the like. On the Monday before Good Friday, Jesus chased the money changers out of the temple for exchanging currency for a premium. The Bible declares:

> And they come to Jerusalem: and Jesus went into the temple, and began to cast out them that sold and bought in the temple, and overthrew the tables of the moneychangers, and the seats of them that sold doves; And would not suffer that any man should carry any vessel through the temple. (Mark 11:15-16)

Not only are selling and commercializing unbiblical, they take away time that could be spent on the weightier matters of church growth, such as evangelism.

Notice, no vessel was allowed to be carried through the temple. Vessels represent anything that might be sold for a profit. The church is not a profit-making organization. I am not suggesting, however, that the church should not teach good work ethics. For example, allowing the young people to provide a service to the community by having a car wash, or the church having a separate 501(c)(3) corporation for the purpose of economic development and job training is a beneficial thing. This is not what I am addressing. I am addressing the practice of raising the operating budget by selling products and merchandising. Jesus said,

"My house shall be called of all nations the house of prayer, but ye have made it a den of thieves." (Mark 11:17)

There is sin in the house. Not only are selling and commercializing unbiblical, they take away time that could be spent on the weightier matters of church growth, such as evangelism. When we are preoccupied with raising money by profitable selling, we omit other church growth principles and remain victims to the crucial problem that I have labeled "cursed giving."

If it is perceived that the pastor, stewardship committee, or trustees have no accountability, giving is faced with a roadblock.

SOLUTION TWO: *Change negative perceptions that prohibit giving.*

Perceptions are real in the mind of the perceiver. There are negative perceptions fostered by churches and church leaders that prohibit giving. For example, it is perceived that the pastor or the church mishandles money. This prohibits giving.

If it is perceived that the pastor, stewardship committee, or trustees have no accountability, giving is faced with a roadblock. Clear cut published procedures should be made in an attempt to change any negative perception that would bar the potential for giving. Perceptions come from many avenues. Explore all avenues and do everything possible to change a negative perception to a positive perception.

The following are some relative suggestions on how you might change negative perceptions that prohibit to positive perceptions that encourage giving:

A. Involve the whole church in the budget planning process.

A few people should not plan the entire budget only to be voted on by the congregation. Rather, all the ministries of the church, through their respective leaders, should have input into the budget planning process from its beginning to its end. Budget fairs or budget expositions can further help involve the entire congregation in the budget process.

B. Adopt a unified budget.

A unified budget is a budget wherein all the funds are managed under one umbrella account. Too many accounts lead to perceptions of mishandling funds, thus barring uninhibited giving.

C. Adopt and implement, through a regular reporting process, a full disclosure policy and procedure on all money received and spent.

D. Shield clergy from the appearance of doing evil relative to the handling of money in the church.

The church that I pastor has an operating budget that has grown from $30,000 to over $3,500,000 in twenty years. I do not handle any money, count any money, or write or sign any checks. In other words, my hands do not touch the money. However, I have not given up my pastoral responsibility of overseeing the stewardship of the church. I oversee via reports, spreadsheets, etc., but I do not touch the money. The clergy are often perceived, particularly by the lost and unchurched, as flock fleecers. When clergy do not handle the money, it goes a long way in helping change the perception and appearance that there is sin in the house.

...when the congregation knows that the pastor is well compensated, it eliminates the perception of him/her being greedy, as well as puts to rest the wondering of whether the pastor is getting some extra amount.

E. Pay the pastor an above average well-published salary.

The scripture clearly teaches that a servant is worthy of his hire (Luke 10:7). A good pastor is the most valuable asset any church can possess. Teaching this truth to the congregation will help clean the house. Also, when the congregation knows that the pastor is well compensated, it eliminates the perception of him/her being greedy, as well as puts to rest the wondering of whether the pastor is getting some extra amount.

In addition, the pastor is freed from the worries of how he is going to take care of his family. He can give ample time and energy to taking care of the congregation.

SOLUTION THREE: *Promote and implement a steward-ship revival at least once a year that addresses the theme and question of, "What Does the Bible Say About Giving?"*

John 15:3 records,

> Now ye are clean through the word which I have spoken unto you.

God's word can deliver the church from the crucial problems of cursed giving. The word, however, must be rightly divided. The word must be taught under the anointing of the Holy Spirit. Seek that anointing, or seek someone who has that special anointing, to rightly divide God's word about money. Hosea states,

> My people are destroyed for lack of knowledge. (Hosea 4:6)

If the church does not know, the church will remain under the curse. However, knowledge of God's word will break the curse.

SOLUTION FOUR: *Commit to percentage giving rather than a dollar amount.*

First of all, *commit*. Don't be afraid to ask for commit-ments. One of the core values of Greenforest Community Baptist Church states: "I believe that a personal demon-strative commitment is a powerful Christian witness. This includes annually signing commitment cards concerning the giving of our time, gifts, talents and money." One of

Percentage commitments help foster sacrificial giving and eliminate competitive giving.

the reasons that the world is making a mockery of the church is because of our apparent lack of commitment.

The tithe involves percentage giving. Percentage giving allows for equal sacrifice rather than equal contributions. Equal giving is unfair and unbiblical. The scripture of the widow's mites clearly teaches the lesson of sacrificial giving (Luke 21:1-4). Percentage commitments help foster sacrificial giving and eliminate competitive giving.

Commitment is a biblical precept. We are a covenant people, and we serve a covenant God; therefore, we should be a committed people. A covenant is a binding agreement between two or more parties. After entering the promised land, Joshua, like the patriarchs that came before him and others who came after him, led the people in a covenant relationship with God (Joshua 24:25).

Christ, through the Cross and the shedding of His blood, represents a New Covenant (Testament). A commitment represents our portion of a covenant. A commitment to sacrificial percentage giving will go a long way to help eradicate the sin of cursed giving.

SOLUTION FIVE: *Teach stewardship in its entirety.*

Stewardship involves more than simply giving money. Stewardship involves the proper use of our time, talents, gifts, and money. Stewardship involves more

The first step in being delivered from cursed giving is to acknowledge that God owns everything.

than tithing. Stewardship involves not only a tenth, but also the other ninety.

The first step in being delivered from cursed giving is to acknowledge that God owns everything. He is creator and we are creature. It all belongs to God.

SOLUTION SIX: *Teach all of the biblical principles of giving.*

To solve the problem of cursed giving, we must teach all the principles of giving. There are at least four prominent principles of giving that the scriptures teach.

First, there is the principle of "first fruits" giving. We are to give first to God before we give anywhere else (Deuteronomy 18:4). We are to give Him our best, the strength of our youth.

Second, there is the principle of purposeful giving. The scripture teaches us that we are to plan what we give to the church. We should not give haphazardly. Second Corinthians 9:7 states:

> "Every man according as he purposeth in his heart, so let him give; not grudgingly, or of necessity; for God loveth a cheerful giver."

Many Christians do not decide what they are going to give on Sunday morning until it comes time to collect the offering. That is not purposeful giving. We see this in ourselves when we reach into our pockets at the last minute and make

Legalistic giving and begrudged giving help foster the sin in the house.

a decision as to what we are going to give from our pockets at that time, and what we might want to spend on dinner after church. This type of giving clearly violates God's principle of "first fruit" giving and enhances sin in the house.

Third, the Bible teaches the principle of "willful" giving. The Lord loves a cheerful giver. Giving with the wrong motives can cancel your blessing. Giving out of duty or obligation is giving legalistically. Jesus told the Pharisees in Matthew 23.23 that they do indeed tithe, but they ought to also show mercy and faith. Legalistic giving and begrudged giving help foster the sin in the house. Giving out of love, willingly and cheerfully, helps eliminate the problem associated with cursed giving.

Fourth, is the principle of "sacrificial" giving. Sacrificial giving means giving up something. In baseball, an often used strategy is called a sacrifice play. The batter is asked to give up his opportunity to be a star, hit a home run, or add to his personal batting average by executing a sacrificial bunt designed to advance another player. The batter gives of himself for the good of the team.

When we sacrificially give to God, we give up some of our personal desires, wants, and even needs, for the betterment of the body of Christ and the Kingdom of God. Jesus told the Pharisees, concerning the widow who gave two mites,

that this poor widow hath cast in more than they all:
For all these have of their abundance cast in unto the

offerings of God: but she of her penury hath cast in all the living that she had. (Luke 21:3,4)

Sacrificial giving can be seen in the divine wisdom of God's tithe. Giving a percentage, or tenth, promotes equal sacrifice regardless of available income. Failing to give sacrificially adds to the sin in the house. Giving sacrificially cleanses the house.

SOLUTION SEVEN: *Devise a plan whereby members can systematically grow to the tithe.*

Tithing is an issue of faith and not a matter of money. All believers are not at the same level of faith. However, God has promised that if we have a little faith (as a grain of mustard seed), He will provide the increase.

We may become believers instantaneously, but we certainly don't become disciples instantaneously.

And Jesus said unto them, Because of your unbelief: for verily I say unto you, If ye have faith as a grain of mustard seed, ye shall say unto this mountain, Remove hence to yonder place; and it shall remove; and nothing shall be impossible unto you. (Matthew 17:20)

We are called to grow in our discipleship. We may become believers instantaneously, but we certainly don't become disciples instantaneously. We grow to become disciples. A disciple is a tither. A believer may or may not be. All believers should become disciples. Disciples are trained believers. Therefore, believers should be given an opportunity to grow in giving.

There is no reason why a believer should not be allowed to grow into a tither, especially if the believer will be obedient to the other principles of giving just mentioned, which require more obedience than faith. It requires only a little faith to be obedient to the four biblical principles, namely (1) firstfruits; (2) purposeful; (3) willful; and (4) sacrificial giving. Churches that encourage believers to grow to tithing disciples will eventually be delivered from the sin of cursed giving.

SOLUTION EIGHT: *Teach that Jesus was a tither.*

If we are disciples (learners and followers) of Jesus, we must know His behavior. If Jesus was not a tither then I am not required to be a tither because I am a follower/disciple of Him. Jesus was a tither and He commanded us to be tithers.

In Matthew 23:23, Jesus told the Pharisees and us:

> Woe unto you, scribes and Pharisees, hypocrites! for ye pay tithe of mint and anise and cummin, and have omitted the weightier matters of the law, judgment, mercy, and faith: these ought ye to have done, and not to leave the other undone.

How many times does God have to tell us what to do and what not to do? Prayerfully, only once. In this scripture Jesus says you ought to tithe. Jesus did not reprimand the Pharisees for tithing. He reprimanded them for not showing love and mercy. Speaking of the tithe, Jesus says,

Jesus was a tither. If we are to follow Him, then the members of His body (the Church) must be tithers. Anything less precipitates sin in the house.

"for ye pay tithe." Jesus was a tither. Why do I believe that Jesus was a tither?

I believe Jesus was a tither because, in the New Testament, He continuously confronts the Pharisees. He never criticizes them for tithing and they never criticized Him for not tithing. In His continuing saga of New Testament episodes, He never condemned their tithing. The Pharisees were committed and staunch tithers. They tithed everything, even down to the herbs in their garden. This world be the equivalent today of tithing the tomatoes we may have planted in our backyards and on our patios.

Jesus did criticize and condemn them for other things, however, such as being hypocrites, saying long meaningless prayers, not showing justice, mercy, and love, but never once did He ever condemn them for not tithing. More significantly, in their zealous quest to disarm and defame Jesus, they never accused Him of not being a tither.

The Pharisees accused Jesus of breaking and not honoring the religious orders, such as healing on the Sabbath, not ritualistically washing, eating with sinners, but they never accused Him of not being a tither. Jesus was a tither. If we are to follow Him, then the members of His body (the Church) must be tithers. Anything less precipitates sin in the house.

Skull Practice
CHAPTER ONE — CURSED GIVING

1. What does scripture say about being cursed for not tithing?

   Answer: Ye are cursed with a curse: for ye have robbed me, even the whole nation (Malachi 3:9).

2. What is your relationship with God if you are not a tither?

   Answer: If you are not a tither you are outside the will of God; therefore, your relationship with God is less than perfect.

3. Do we rob God?

   Answer: Yes! We rob God every Sunday morning when we are disobedient to God's commandment to tithe.

4. Is failing to tithe a sin?

   Answer: Yes! Failure to do anything God tells us to do is a sin. God commands us to tithe.

Fill in the blanks

1. "Bring ye all of the _____ into the storehouse." (tithes)

2. God tells us that we are blessed when we _____.
   (tithe)

3. God tells us that we are cursed when we do not
   _____. (tithe)

4. The _____ promotes equal sacrifice and not
   equal giving. (tithe)

5. Jesus was a _____. (tither)

Helpful Dialogue

1. The church should engage in an act of "Church
   Reform" rather than being so concerned with "Welfare
   Reform." If all Christians were tithers, this nation
   would not need a welfare system.

2. If we multiply the average income per family times the
   number of church families or adult members, we can
   determine the buying power of any given church. What
   will happen if this problem remains?

   If we take ten percent of that number we can determine
   what the church budget should be if every member
   were a tither. If we subtract that number from the actual yearly income of the church, we can put a dollar figure to the amount of sin in the church. Using these
   guidelines we can determine:

   (1) What should be the buying power of your church;

(2) What your budget should be if everyone were a tither; and

(3) A dollar figure on how much sin is in your church.

3. Selling is not God's way of supporting the ministries of the church. If your church is still depending upon selling to support the church, what would happen if you decided to be obedient to God and support the church God's way?

4. Involving the whole church in the budgeting process helps promote tithing and good overall stewardship in general. What are some of the individual and group dynamics that are involved in this process? How can more people in your church become involved in the budget process? What do you think the results will be?

What Will Happen If the Problem Is Not Resolved?

1. You will never be truly blessed.

2. The spiritual and numerical growth of the church will be stifled.

3. You will not be in a perfect relationship with God.

4. You will remain cursed with a curse.

CHAPTER TWO

Carnal Secular Thinking

A major problem of church growth is that churches have permitted secular thinking to determine their methods of operation.

Proverbs 3:5–6 is one of the often quoted Old Testament scriptures. Many claim it to be their favorite. "Trust in the LORD with all thine heart; and lean not unto thine own understanding. In all thy ways acknowledge him, and he shall direct thy paths."

Yet one of the greatest sin problems of the church is the abuse of this scripture. More often than not, we lean on our own understanding. Leaning on our own understanding is carnal. Leaning on our own understanding results in secular thinking. Secular thinking is one of the carnal sins in the house. When we move away from scripture, we move ever so closely to the garbage heap of carnal thinking.

A major problem of church growth is that churches have permitted secular thinking to determine their methods of operation. We have adopted secular procedures for a church environment. We must first understand that the ways of the world stand contrary to biblical principles. For example, the world values rugged individualism. Yet God calls us to be an army. The world esteems independence. Yet God calls us to be dependent on Him and, at least, interdependent on each other. The world values competition and aggressiveness, but God calls us to be compassionate and humble. Our society values self. God calls us to deny self.

Trustee is not a biblical term of office.

We live in a democracy, and I, for one, am happy to be living under a democratic form of government. Yet I see no biblical reference or scriptural inference that the church should be a democracy. I believe that the church is not a democracy. Rather, it is a theocracy. Being a theocracy means that God rules. This is not some ideology that cannot be implemented. We can govern the church God's way. Nowhere in the Bible do we find governing boards. Yet, our churches are top-heavy with deacon boards, trustee boards, etc. _Trustee_ is not a biblical term of office. Yet, our churches are often governed by trustee boards.

Please know that I have nothing against boards or the fine well-meaning people who serve on boards. I personally serve on several boards in the Atlanta area, including the board that rules the City of Atlanta transportation system, MARTA (Metropolitan Atlanta Rapid Transit Authority). People who serve on boards can be the finest people in the world, but the fact remains that boards, by their very nature, are legalistic. Boards operate according to the letter of the law and the church should operate according to the spirit of love. I don't think it was an oversight on God's part not to mention boards in the Bible, although He clearly taught about elders, as well as the deacons and pastors being the only chief officers of the church.

On a somewhat sarcastic, and maybe facetious note, many churches clearly have in their bylaws that their business meetings will be operated according to *Robert's Rules of Order*. Yet very few of us know who Mr. Robert is, and none of us knows if Mr. Robert was saved. Why then, are we operating our business meetings according to him? Maybe that is one reason why our church business meetings have been nightmares and damage so many Christian lives. The point of all this is that because of secular thinking, we have sought to operate our churches and make church decisions based on our own understanding, rather than acknowledge Him in all our ways and allow Him to direct our path. Thus, sin is in the house.

A BIBLICAL ILLUSTRATION FROM THE CORINTHIAN CHURCH

God speaks to us through Paul and the church at Corinth about secular thinking. Paul opens the third chapter of 1 Corinthians by calling the church carnal for their worldly behavior:

> For ye are yet carnal: for whereas there is among you envying, and strife, and divisions, are ye not carnal, and walk as men? (1 Corinthians 3:3)

Paul closes this third chapter by rebuking carnal thinking:

> Let no man deceive himself. If any man among you seemeth to be wise in this world, let him become a fool, that he may be wise. For the wisdom of this world is foolishness with God. For it is written, He taketh the wise in their own craftiness. And again, the Lord knoweth the thoughts of the wise, that they are vain. (1 Corinthians 3:18-20)

Keep in mind that at this point in the life of the church, Paul is not rebuking them for immorality, though the city of Corinth was plagued with immorality. One of the major influences in the city was the Temple of Aphrodite, the goddess of love. Temple prostitutes are reported to have performed sexual rituals and acts within the confines of the Temple. I would imagine that many of the members of the newly formed Corinthian church had once visited and participated in the rituals of the Temple. But by the power of God, they had been called out of that immoral environment and for the most part had cleaned up their moral lives. They had not, however, been delivered and cleaned from the sin of carnal thinking. Therefore, there was division in the church at Corinth.

A careful reading of this text reveals that Paul did not question their salvation. Paul felt that he had laid down for them a solid foundation.

> For other foundation can no man lay than that is
> laid, which is Jesus Christ. (1 Corinthians 3:11)

The challenge for the Corinthian church, as well as for
us, is to be careful how we build on that solid foundation.
If we build with weaker material such as wood, hay, and
straw, our work will be burned and much will be lost,
although we will be saved. However, if we build on the
foundation with gold, silver and precious stone at the time
of judgment we will be rewarded.

> Now if any man build upon this foundation gold,
> silver, precious stones, wood, hay, stubble; Every
> man's work shall be made manifest: for the day
> shall declare it, because it shall be revealed by fire;
> and the fire shall try every man's work of what sort
> it is. If any man's work abide which he hath built
> thereupon, he shall receive a reward. If any man's
> work shall be burned, he shall suffer loss: but he
> himself shall be saved; yet so as by fire. (1
> Corinthians 3:12-15)

Since, at this point in the life of the Corinthian church,
immorality was not the major problem; and because Paul
opens and closes this chapter speaking of worldly and
wise thinking, I believe these poor building materials
could refer to carnal and secular thinking. Wood, hay, and
straw represent leaning on your own understanding,
which is carnal and will produce negative results. Gold,
precious stone and silver represent discerning the will of
Christ, resulting in positive results. Likewise, building
God's kingdom and growing churches using the materials

of secular and carnal thinking will produce negative results. Building God's kingdom and growing churches using the material of the best interpretation of the word of God, and the best spiritual discernment of the likeness of Christ, will result in positive results. How can this be done? The following are some tried and proved suggestions for your consideration.

HOUSE CLEANING SOLUTIONS

SOLUTION ONE: *Study the Mind of Christ with an Emphasis on Obeying the Mind of Christ*

The scripture addresses us concerning the mind of Christ:

> Let this mind be in you, which was also in Christ Jesus. (Philippians 2:5)

Notice that this suggestion emphasizes obeying the mind of Christ, not just knowing the mind of Christ. First, we must know, then we must obey. Knowing represents the first half of the Great Commission:

> Go ye therefore, and teach all nations, baptizing them in the name of the Father, and of the Son, and of the Holy Ghost. (Matthew 28:19)

Obeying represents the second half of the Great Commission:

> Teaching them to observe all things whatsoever I have commanded you: and, lo, I am with you alway, even unto the end of the world. Amen. (Matthew 28:20)

Teaching church members to obey the mind of Christ means teaching them to vote only the mind of Christ in church business meetings, rather than voting their opinion (leaning on their own understanding).

Often we know, but we don't obey. The focus of this book is to bring the church into conformity with the scriptures. To do so we must observe (obey) all its statutes and commandments. Teaching church members to obey the mind of Christ means teaching them to vote only the mind of Christ in church business meetings, rather than voting their opinion (leaning on their own understanding).

SOLUTION TWO: *Teach and Emphasize the Contemporary Manifestation of the Priesthood of Believers.*

The doctrine of the priesthood of believers is basically embraced by all Protestant churches. In essence, we Protestants believe that when Jesus died on the cross and the curtain was torn in the Temple, all believers were given access to God in and through our Intercessor, Jesus.

And the sun was darkened, and the veil of the temple was rent in the midst. (Luke 23:45)

Therefore, we are a priesthood of believers. We are not, however, priests in and within ourselves. But we have become priests in and through Jesus. What are the church

...because we are priests through Jesus, we no longer have the privilege of our own opinions on church issues.

related implications? And how is our priesthood lived out (manifested) in the church today.

Once again, I believe that because we are priests through Jesus, we no longer have the privilege of our own opinions on church issues. What we do have is the glorious privilege to approach the throne of God to seek His will and to cast a vote on His behalf. Our self-seeking thinking has put a lid on the kingdom building and church growth. Implementing the doctrine of the priesthood of believers would help kick the lids off the church and clean up the sin of secular and carnal thinking.

SOLUTION THREE: *Replace Business Meetings with Holy Spirit Discernment Sessions.*

To some this may seem to be simply a play on words or a matter of semantics. I believe not. I believe that the implementation of this suggestion will provide an opportunity for churches to practice Suggestion One "Being of the mind of Christ" and Suggestion Two, the application of the "priesthood of believers" doctrine.

Historically, business meetings have been the major church event wherein secular and carnal thinking have been most damaging. There are thousands of wounded Christians who have been victimized by the way we

Historically, business meetings have been the major church event wherein secular and carnal thinking have been most damaging.

conduct business in the church. This is the epitome of sin in the house. Something must be done to eradicate this problem. If believers would come to business meetings with the heart of the priesthood of believers and with the mind of Christ, with the understanding that it is a privilege to discern the will of God and cast a vote on His behalf, the sin of secular and carnal thinking in business meetings would be erased.

SOLUTION FOUR: *Consider a Boardless Form of Church Government*

I am not suggesting that we eliminate deacons, elders, or any other biblical position of the church. But I am suggesting that we replace boards with ministries. It is possible that the same people could serve on the ministry teams that currently serve on the board, and be given some of the same decision-making assignments. However, a ministry's focus is drastically different from a board's focus. Ministries are focused on the spirit of love. Boards focus on the spirit of the law.

Clearly, in gospel, grace is supreme to law. Can a church operate with integrity without boards? Yes! Also, the fastest growing churches today do not have boards. I am not sure that they have more integrity, but they certainly don't have less integrity than board-operated

Boards tend to board-up the church; ministries tend to blow the tops off the church.

churches. Boards tend to board-up the church; ministries tend to blow the tops off the church. The top is blown off because the bureaucracy and red tape that have kept the top nailed down have been removed. God wants the top off. Boards represent the nails that keep the top on. Ministries tend to seek the mind of Christ; boards more often than not tend to foster secular and carnal thinking that perpetuate sin in the house.

SOLUTION FIVE: *Bring the Church Bylaws into Conformity with Scripture*

The reality is that many church members are more familiar with the church bylaws than they are with biblical truths. The reality of this fact is evidence of the sin of secular thinking. Historically, members are more familiar with the bylaws of the church (able to quote articles and sections from memory) because the bylaws represent an instrument of control. Bylaws help control and maintain the status quo. They are loved and oftentimes worshiped by secular thinkers. However, church bylaws can become a positive change agent of the church. The key is to bring the bylaws into conformity with scripture. In order to do this, bylaw revisions must occur.

In the church that I pastor, we have had four major revisions in twenty years. Remember, from a legal standpoint, the bylaws need only to contain those things that a bank would need for a loan or the state would need for incor-

Every effort should be made to revise the bylaws to reflect biblical truths.

poration. All the other content, such as operational and administrative procedures, are internal, and they may or may not be necessary. Those things that fall into the above categories should come into conformity with scripture.

Every effort should be made to revise the bylaws to reflect biblical truths. Bringing the bylaws into conformity with scripture will definitely help the church overcome and conquer the sin of carnal secular thinking.

Skull Practice
CHAPTER TWO — CARNAL SECULAR THINKING

1. Is secular thinking a sin?
   Yes, as it relates to issues and concerns of the church. God's word should govern the church as well as our spiritual lives.

2. Are there any governing boards found in the Bible?
   No!

3. Are there trustees in the Bible?
   No!

4. Are there elders in the Bible?
   Yes!

Fill in the Blanks

1. Leaning on our own understanding is _____. (carnal thinking)

2. One of the major carnal sins in the house (church) is _____. (carnal thinking)

3. When we move away from scripture, we move closer to the garbage heap of _____. (carnal thinking)

4. In 1 Corinthians, chapter 3, in the opening and closing verses, God uses His servant, Paul, to rebuke _____. (carnal thinking)

5. Much of the confusion and tension that is manifested in church business meetings is the result of _____ _____ _____. (carnal secular thinking)

6. Knowing the mind of Christ (Philippians 2:5) will help cleanse the sin of _____ _____ _____. (carnal secular thinking)

Helpful Dialogue

1. One of the major problems in the church is that members and leaders have adopted secular procedures for the church environment. Is this true in your church? In what area of the church do you see this problem manifested? How has this been detrimental to the life of the church?

2. The secular world in general stands contrary to many biblical principles. For example, the secular world values self, but God calls us to deny self. What are some examples of this? What are the implications relative to the life of the church?

3. The church is a theocracy, which means that God rules; rather than a democracy, meaning the people rule. How can the doctrine of the priesthood of believ-

ers help resolve the tension between these two forms of government.

4. The church bylaws (constitution) is considered a legal document necessary for incorporation, borrowing money, and other legal matters. How can this legal instrument be utilized as an agent of change for the enhancement of spiritual and numerical growth of the church?

What Will Happen If the Problem Is Not Resolved?

1. You will always walk in the flesh and not in the Spirit.

2. You will forfeit the power of the Holy Spirit working in your life and the life of the church.

3. You will not live the abundant life for which Jesus died.

4. The church will turn people away and run people away, as opposed to bringing people in and keeping people in.

CHAPTER THREE

Stuck on Salvation

The greatest gift of God has become one of the crucial church growth problems.

Stuck means you are not moving. It implies that something is keeping you from moving. You are stuck in the mud, stuck in traffic, stuck on yourself, or stuck in or on something. What a tragedy! The greatest gift of God has become one of the crucial church growth problems. Christian churches are stuck on salvation.

Stuck on salvation means refusing to grow in Christ after the point of conversion. Jesus came and died on the cross for the gift of salvation. The gift of love is the gift of salvation. One of His seven last words on the cross was, "It is finished." He was saying the unfolding redemptive work of salvation is finished. Nothing else on God's part needed to be done. "It is finished" referred to the completion of the plan of salvation. However, Jesus said, "It is finished," not "I am finished." Jesus is not finished. As a matter of fact, He went to work on the day He died. He descended into the depths of hell to preach to the captives.

Now that he ascended, what is it but that he also descended first into the lower parts of the earth? (Ephesians 4:9)

By which also he went and preached unto the spirits in prison. (1 Peter 3:19)

There is work to do. There is the unfinished business of the cross.

He continued His work on Sunday by rising from the dead. He worked forty more days before He ascended into heaven. Jesus is working in the world today in the person of the Holy Spirit, and He is coming again to judge the living and the dead. Jesus' work did not stop on the cross with salvation, and neither can ours. We are His colaborers. There is work to do. There is the unfinished business of the cross. We were not only saved from something—we were saved for something. We are saved to serve.

It is interesting how we quote Ephesians 2:8, 9, and fail to quote verse 10:

(8) For by grace are ye saved through faith; and that not of yourselves: it is the gift of God: (9) Not of works, lest any man should boast. (10) For we are his workmanship, created in Christ Jesus unto good works, which God hath before ordained that we should walk in them.

We are His workmanship. God both created us and ordained us to serve.

Yet many churches today are stuck on salvation. We have missed the mark of service. Missing the mark is defined as sin. There is sin in the house when we fail to do our part as co-laborers with Him. Before Jesus ascended into heaven He gave the church some marching orders. The instructions are clear:

> Go ye therefore, and teach all nations, baptizing them in the name of the Father, and of the Son, and of the Holy Ghost: Teaching them to observe all things whatsoever I have commanded you: and, lo, I am with you alway, even unto the end of the world. Amen. (Matthew 28:19-20)

Notice that Jesus told us to "make" disciples. In the Greek text, "make" is the only verb of command in the sentence.

> Therefore go and make disciples of all nations, baptizing them in the name of the Father and of the Son and of the Holy Spirit. (Matthew 28:19, NIV)

Many churches are doing everything *but* making disciples.

Our instructions are to make disciples. Many churches are doing everything *but* making disciples. A disciple is a disciplined learner and devoted follower. They are few in number, even in mega-churches.

Discipleship involves growing up in the likeness of Christ. Many churches are top heavy and over loaded with babes in Christ. Our membership is plagued with bottle-carrying, diaper-

wearing Christians. God is tired of babysitting and changing diapers. The Holy Spirit is grieved:

> And grieve not the holy Spirit of God, whereby
> ye are sealed unto the day of redemption.
> (Ephesians 4:30)

...many churches are dysfunctional, and there are many wounded dysfunctional Christians.

It is time to clean the house. It is time to grow up. In another book I authored entitled, *Growing Up to the Head* (Orman Press, 1997), I present the picture of the church as a weak body with a perfect Head. The Church is the body of Christ, and Christ is the Head of the body. The body is weak, but the head is perfect. This causes a functional operational problem. The problem is that the body cannot carry out the instructions given by the head. Therefore, many churches are dysfunc-tional, and there are many wounded, dysfunctional Christians. God is calling the Church, in these latter days, to grow up and rejoice in our salvation, but not to become stuck on it.

A Biblical Illustration

Luke's gospel illustrates a life of stewardship referred to as the parable of the pounds. The pound represents all that which God has given us to manage for Him until He returns. The pounds represent tools, talents, or gifts for the task of ministry. God gave three servants ten pounds each. Upon His return He asked them to report on their usage of the pounds. Two of the servants had done well. God said to them:

Well, thou good servant: because thou hast been faithful in a very little, have thou authority over ten cities. (Luke 19:17)

But the other servant had kept his stewardship in a napkin and done nothing. This disturbed God greatly, and He said:

And he saith unto him, Out of thine own mouth will I judge thee, thou wicked servant. Thou knewest that I was an austere man, taking up that I laid not down, and reaping that I did not sow: Wherefore then gavest not thou my money into the bank, that at my coming I might have required mine own with usury? And he said unto them that stood by, Take from him the pound, and give it to him that hath ten pounds. (Luke 19:22-24)

Many churches have salvation stuffed in a zip-lock® bag, stashed in a freezer, waiting on the rapture.

I believe that stewardship wrapped in a napkin is an accurate analogy to describe how we are stuck on salvation. I believe that the church has her salvation wrapped in a napkin or handkerchief, waiting on the day of redemption. Many churches have salvation stuffed in a zip-lock® bag, stashed in a freezer, waiting on the rapture.

God has gifted us for the unfinished business of the cross. Being stuck on salvation denies the utilization of the spiritual gift God has given each believer for the task of ministry and the edifying of the body.

> Wherefore he saith, When he ascended up on high, he led captivity captive, and gave gifts unto men. (Ephesians 4:8)

Spiritual gifts will seek employment.

God told us in 1 Corinthians 12:1 and 2 Timothy 1:6 not to be ignorant concerning spiritual gifts and to stir up the gift. Being stuck on salvation definitely puts us in disobedience concerning spiritual gifts for the task of ministry. It is a sin to deny God's word. One reason why some churches are growing and other churches are not is that growing churches employ the spiritual gifts of God. Spiritual gifts will seek employment. If they don't find employment at the church, they will look for employment elsewhere. The scripture declares:

> A man's gift maketh room for him, and bringeth him before great men. (Proverb 18:16)

God took the one pound from the unfaithful servant and gave it to the most faithful servant. The implication is that many churches are losing members because they are not fruitful in employing the spiritual gifts that have been given the church.

The gift of life is salvation. However, we must remember that the gift not only includes eternal life later, but abundant life now. Salvation is also existen-

tial. Salvation should be used and not stored. Stored salvation is an indication that the church has gone to sleep at
the gospel plow. In the Garden of Gethsemane Jesus
asked the disciples to watch and pray while He went a little further.

> Then cometh Jesus with them unto a place called
> Gethsemane, and saith unto the disciples, Sit ye
> here, while I go and pray yonder. And he went a lit-
> tle further, and fell on his face, and prayed, saying,
> O my Father, if it be possible, let this cup pass from
> me: nevertheless not as I will, but as thou wilt.
> (Matthew 26:36, 39)

Jesus went a little further so He could fulfill the will of
God. Likewise, we must go a little further in discipleship
and spiritual growth if we are to do the will of God. We
must not fall asleep on the commandment to "make disciples."

Stored salvation is not the will of God. We have been
saved for the glory of life everlasting, but also for the task
of building His kingdom by growing His church until the
day of His return. Let us not be carnal in our going, but
let us proceed in the Spirit and not be guilty of the problem of being stuck on salvation.

HOUSECLEANING SOLUTIONS
SOLUTION ONE: *Implement a Gift-based Ministry.*

A gift-based ministry is more than a class on spiritual
gifts. A gift-based ministry is an ongoing church process
for employing and utilizing the supernatural gifts given

to the believers for the task of ministry. Every believer has been given at least one spiritual gift at the moment of knowing grace (salvation).

> But unto every one of us is given grace according to the measure of the gift of Christ. (Ephesians 4:7)

The role of leadership is to provide a definitive path for those who follow.

These spiritual gifts were given for a purpose. They are not to be stored, misused, or abused. Rather, they are given for the edification of the church. The church has the responsibility to release and utilize this power. Failure to do so in some manner will cause the church to miss the mark. In *Stir Up the Gifts*, another book I have written, there is a chapter entitled "How to Start a Gift-based Ministry in Your Church."

SOLUTION TWO: *Institute a Clear Cut Growth Path for Church Members to Follow.*

The role of leadership is to provide a definitive path for those who follow. Many churches fail to provide, or fail to communicate the expected course to follow for growth. An expected growth course involves much more than having Sunday School or Bible Study class and expecting believers to attend. Rather, there should be a progressive systematic plan of growth established, monitored, and reinforced with achievement awards at intervals along the way. This expectation should be communicated often and with clarity.

Failure to implement this suggestion will leave the majority of churches wandering through the wilderness of curriculums and Bible classes that often will result in a decline in growth and eventually a stoppage. Stopping causes us to become stuck. Getting stuck causes disobedience. Disobedience is missing the mark; and missing the mark is sin. The final outcome is sin in the house.

SOLUTION THREE: *List Spiritual Growth Expectations in Measurable Terms.*

This may seem academic, but I believe listing spiritual growth expectations in measurable terms will help solve spiritual growth stagnation. One of the issues associated with being stuck on salvation centers around the question, How do you measure spiritual growth?

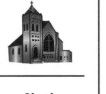

...listing spiritual growth expectations in measurable terms will help solve spiritual growth stagnation.

Granted, that which is spiritual cannot be confined or delineated intellectually. Spirit cannot be measured objectively. However, we can do our best to discern God's will and the outcome of doing God's will. We, therefore, can define it, according to our best scriptural interpretation of how the outcomes of spiritual growth are demonstrated.

If we can define it we can measure it. For example, a level of spiritual growth is reached when 100 percent of the leadership are tithers. Spiritual growth has occurred when 80 percent of the congregation has signed up to work in a ministry task. Listing growth expectation in measurable terms will help us evaluate our spiritual growth. Some churches may not be stuck on salvation. Some may be more stuck than others. If we can objectively measure our spiritual growth we will be able to evaluate where we are and where we need to go. For sure, to stay where we are is not the will of God, and not doing His will is disobedience. Disobedience is sin.

Skull Practice
CHAPTER THREE — STUCK ON SALVATION

1. What is the greatest gift (the gift of life)?
   The gift of life is salvation.

2. What did Jesus mean on the cross in his last words, "It is finished"?
   He meant that the unfolding redemptive work of salvation is finished.

3. What is meant by the statement, "We are not only saved from something, we are also saved for something."
   It means that we are saved from hell, and we are saved to serve on earth.

Fill in the Blanks

1. Refusing to grow in Christ after the time of conversion means that you are _____ ____ _____. (stuck on salvation)

2. The gift of love is the gift of _____. (salvation)

3. Because the church is stuck on salvation, it has missed the mark. Missing the mark is defined as _____. (sin)

4. The command verb in the Great Commission instructs us to _____ disciples. (make)

5. The gift of _____ not only includes eternal life later but abundant life now. (salvation)

6. Stored _____ is not the will of God. (salvation)

Helpful Dialogue

1. Numerical church growth is easily and objectively measured. Spiritual growth, however, cannot really be objectively measured. Yet it is our desire to grow spiritually. Discuss some indicators that might help determine whether a church is growing spiritually.

2. We are saved by grace through faith, and not by works. But we are also told that we are His workmanship created for good works (Ephesians 2:10); and we should work out our salvation (Philippians 2:12). As Christians, and as a church, what should we be doing to fulfill what God has asked us to do and be.

3. Many congregations today are establishing what is being referred to as "gift-based ministry." What is gift-based ministry, and how can it help solve one problem of being stuck on salvation.

What Will Happen If the Problem Is Not Resolved?

1. You will not become what you were created to be and what you were saved for.

2. The army of God will be continually weakened due to a lack of soldiers.

3. Christ's church will not be a force in the world due to a lack of Christian disciples.

4. The Church would have failed at implementing Jesus' last commandment, referred to as the Great Commission.

CHAPTER FOUR

Saint Selfishness

It appears that one of the main problems in the church today can simply be labeled as saint selfishness. How is that believers have been elevated from sinner to saint, yet fail to share the experience? How can we be saved and not share the Savior? Why should Jesus be the best kept secret in our community? I believe we saints are selfish. We share bad and good news about secular current events, but we don't share Jesus with nearly the same intensity. It seems that we prefer to keep Jesus to ourselves.

We have lost compassion for the world.

We have lost compassion for the world. The church seems to be caught up in herself. In another book I authored entitled, *Breaking the Huddle* (Orman Press, 1997), the church is compared to a football team in the huddle. The football team huddles to receive instruction for the next play (plan of action). The team then breaks and runs the play (carries out the plan of action).

The church also huddles on Sunday morning and other times to receive inspiration and information, but the church never breaks the huddle. The church simply moves the huddle from the sanctuary to the parking lot, to the job, to committee meetings, choir rehearsals, conferences, seminars, etc. The church selfishly remains huddled in herself.

In football it is impossible to score and win if the team remains in the huddle. Likewise, it is impossible for the church to score and win for Jesus in the huddle. The church must break out of herself to save a lost and dying world. The church knows the game plan (the plan of instruction).

The Bible says Jesus came to seek and save. Seek and saving is the plan of action. The church must break from her comfort zone to seek and save. Failure to do so is failing to follow Jesus. Failing to follow Jesus is failing to be a disciple. Failing to be a disciple is failing to become what He asked of us. This is sin—sin in the house.

WHY ARE WE SELFISH?

Refusing to change in the church just to satisfy our own desires is selfish.

Selfishness is the result of our fleshly nature. We must understand that we are dealing with flesh, and flesh by nature is sinful. Small children are selfish and do not want to share their toys, brother, sister, or parents. Adults are selfish in that they hoard what they have deemed as theirs.

We can see ourselves as selfish when we refuse to change the order of worship or the tempo of church music to become more reachable to a younger generation or to another culture. A larger percentage of each successive generation is not Christian. I believe this is due to the sinful selfishness of the church.

Refusing to change in the church just to satisfy our own desires is selfish. We want to do church the way we like it. We want to sing the songs we like, and sing them way we like to sing them. We want to be happy before we are holy. God has called us to be holy before happy. Yet He has promised us that if we are holy we will be happy. However, due to our fleshly nature, we prefer our happiness over God's holiness.

Christians should be amenable to change. After all, change is the foundation of our Christian faith.

> And be not conformed to this world: but be ye transformed by the renewing of your mind, that ye may prove what is that good, and acceptable, and perfect, will of God. (Romans 12:2)

It is God's will that a transforming change be part of our Christian experience. My testimony is that I know I have been changed. If it were not for change, I would still be playing on the devil's team. But I changed teams. Also, I changed the way I think about who Christ is. I changed the things I do and say. I know I have been changed. If I could not have been changed, I could not have been saved. We need to value change rather than resist it.

We also see selfishness in ourselves when we forget to pray for a lost generation. If we examine our prayer meetings we will find that over 95 percent of our prayers are for older dying saints who are heaven bound. Glory is on their horizon, and Jesus is their savior and friend. A much lesser

In our fleshly, sinful pursuit of happiness, we have lost our love for the world.

percentage of our prayers are for the next generation, who has not accepted Jesus as savior. Heaven is not their home, and hell will be their final destination.

In our fleshly, sinful pursuit of happiness, we have lost our love for the world. Many churches act like John 3:16 says, "For God so loved the church" rather than "God so loved the world." God hates sin, but so loved the world that He sent His son, Jesus, to die that we might have eternal life.

But God commendeth his love toward us, in that, while we were yet sinners, Christ died for us. (Romans 5:8)

While we were yet in the world, God so loved the world! Jesus loved sinners enough to eat with them. When have you formed a relationship with an unsaved person for the purpose of reaching him or her for Christ? We seem to have the mindset of Jonah rather than the heart and likeness of Jesus.

TWO BIBLICAL ILLUSTRATIONS OF SELFISHNESS

Jonah – An Old Testament Example

Remember Jonah? God called Jonah to go preach to the very evil people in the city of Nineveh. Rather, Jonah in disobedience fled in a ship to Tarshish. Finally overtaken by a storm, Jonah was thrown overboard. But God had prepared a big fish to swallow Jonah. After three days and three nights, Jonah was vomited out on dry land to be given another chance to help save the people of the city of Nineveh. This time Jonah was obedient to the will of God, and the people of the city of Nineveh were saved. But Jonah was displeased and angry that God was sparing the city of Nineveh.

Jonah's problem was clearly one of selfishness. Jonah never wanted to preach repentance to the people of Nineveh. Jonah knew of God's gracious mercy, but did not want to share it.

> And he prayed unto the LORD, and said, I pray thee, O LORD, was not this my saying, when I was yet in my country? Therefore I fled before unto Tarshish: for I knew that thou art a gracious God, and merciful, slow to anger, and of great kindness, and repentest thee of the evil. (Jonah 4:2)

Jonah knew of God's goodness, but did not want the people of Nineveh to know of His goodness. Jonah was selfish. We, like Jonah, are selfish. We have witnessed the goodness of God. We have experienced the grace and mercy of God. We sing about it and rejoice in it, but fail to share it. To do so is selfish and perpetuates sin. God wants to teach us a lesson like He taught Jonah. God prepared a gourd to protect Jonah from sun and wind. Then God sent a worm to eat up the gourd. When the sun came Jonah was so hot he prayed to die. God had to remind Jonah of the gourd that he neither worked for nor made. God said:

And should not I spare Nineveh, that great city, wherein are more than sixscore thousand persons that cannot discern between their right hand and their left hand. (Jonah 4:11)

God wants the church to know that His grace is available to all. We should tell everybody about His grace. Keeping something to yourself is selfishness. Selfishness is sin. There is sin in the house.

A New Testament Example – Matthew 27:1-5

I would like to propose that if the religious leaders (chief priests and elders) during the lifetime of Jesus had not been selfish, Judas would not have hung himself. When the chief priests and elders decided to put Jesus to death, Judas tried to repent.

Then Judas, which had betrayed him, when he saw that he was condemned, repented himself, and brought again the thirty pieces of silver to the chief priests and elders, Saying, I have sinned in that I have betrayed the innocent blood. And they said, What is that to us? see thou to that. And he cast down the pieces of silver in the temple, and departed, and went and hanged himself. (Matthew 27:3-5)

What a selfish statement on the part of the religious leaders to proclaim, "What is that to us?"

When we treat society's outcasts with cold shoulders in the church, we are, in effect, saying, "What is it to us?"

"What is it to us?" is a selfish proclamation. Yet it is resounding in our churches today. It epitomizes this sin that exists in the church today.

When we fail to minister to alcoholics, to hard core drug addicts, and to those living with the contemporary leprosy, AIDS, we are saying, "What is it to us?"

When we fail to preach and teach a liberation gospel in our churches we are in essence saying, "What is it to us?"

When we fail to visit the prisons, feed the homeless, and clothe the naked, we are selfishly proclaiming, "What is it to us?"

We, like the priests and scribes, fail in our good Samaritan duties by walking over, passing by, and going around those needing help as we make our way up to our Jerusalems. We are reiterating, "What is it to us?"

"What is it to us?" is a selfish proclamation. Yet it is resounding in our churches today. It epitomizes this sin that exists in the church today.

HOUSE CLEANING SOLUTIONS
SOLUTION ONE: *Put Yourself on a "Mission Diet" and Influence Your Church to Get on a Perpetual "Mission Diet."*

Matthew 16:25 states:

> For whoever wants to save his life will lose it, but whoever loses his life for me will find it. (NIV)

The best cure for selfishness is to give yourself away. Each auxiliary, committee, ministry, small group, etc. of the church should be expected, influenced, and encouraged to spearhead a mission project at least once a year. This includes groups such as the finance committee, trustees, and other decision-making organization that often never get involved in missions.

We can minister to each other, but we cannot mission to each other.

SOLUTION TWO: *Clearly Define and Communicate Missions as "Giving to Others," Rather than "Ministering to Each Other."*

Some churches confuse missions with ministry. We can minister to each other, but we cannot mission to each other. Mission work always takes place outside the local body of Christ. We can observe the manifestation of the problem of confusion by reviewing our church budget line items. Monies that are used in any way to serve the local body of Christ should not be designated as missions. For example, monies for the local church's academic school should not be a mission line item.

SOLUTION THREE: *Require Each Ministry to Have and Implement an Evangelistic Component.*

One of the primary purposes of the church is evangelism. Saint selfishness prohibits evangelism. Every ministry of the church should at least have an evangelistic component. For example, some churches have a very

If the ministry does not have an actualized evangelistic component it should either immediately implement one or be eliminated as a ministry of the church.

active recreation and athletic ministry, and there is no evangelistic component.

The purpose of the ministry is not just to play athletics. There must be a planned component that forces the ball to stop bouncing and the game to stop, so that Christ can be lifted up so lost and unchurched people can be reached.

We should examine all of our ministries to determine if there is an actualized evangelistic component. If the ministry does not have such a component, it should either immediately implement one or be eliminated as a ministry of the church. For example, if the music ministry does not have a clear cut plan of evangelism for their concerts, then they should not have a concert. Inviting the pastor to come and extend a call to discipleship after we have massaged ourselves in the goodness of God through music is not an acceptable evangelistic component. The same amount of energy and hard work should be expended to get lost people to come to the concert as is spent in preparing to sing.

SOLUTION FOUR: *Adopt, and Teach, a Church-wide, User-friendly Approach to Sharing Jesus.*

We don't share Jesus because we are selfish. Also, we don't share Jesus because we don't know how or we are fearful. The reason also could be because of a combination of selfishness, ignorance, and fear. Regardless, we must eliminate the ignorance and fearfulness to deal with the root problem of selfishness.

Therefore, churches must provide all members with a user-friendly approach to sharing Jesus.

Churches must provide all members with a user-friendly approach to sharing Jesus. It is likely that a user-friendly approach will not involve the memorization of scripture that selected trained soul-winners employ. Rather, a user-friendly approach should be taught church wide and should facilitate and encourage all members to share Jesus and invite people to church in a non-threatening manner. The objective is to make it more difficult to be selfish and to eliminate all selfish excuses.

The book entitled, *People Sharing Jesus*, by Darrell Robinson, is an excellent source to help establish your approach. Also, at the Greenforest Community Baptist Church, we have implemented an "Andrew and Andrella" ministry. As you know, the biblical character Andrew brought his brother Peter to meet Jesus. Andrella is the name we designated for a female Andrew. Members who simply bring someone to church are recognized and rewarded for being Andrews and Andrellas.

The concept is to share and not be selfish. Sharing and selfishness are incompatible. It is difficult to share and be selfish simultaneously. Sharing Jesus is an excellent antidote for saint selfishness.

Bringing to remembrance the hour we first knew grace, found Jesus, and got saved will wash away selfish instincts.

SOLUTION FIVE: *Teach, Emphasize, Promote, and Encourage Salvation Testimonies.*

Testifying concerning conversion experiences helps combat selfishness. Bringing to remembrance the hour we first knew grace, found Jesus, and got saved will wash away selfish instincts. However, church members must be taught the "what" and "how" of a salvation testimony. There are many kinds of testimonies. We only need to be saved once, but we can be delivered many times from many things.

Every act of mercy, goodness and grace deserves a testimony. However, this suggestion specifically focuses on salvation testimonies that should at least include "My life before salvation," "What happened," and "My life after salvation." This must be taught, encouraged, and promoted. Being able to communicate salvation testimonies may be the best medicine available for saint selfishness.

Skull Practice
CHAPTER FOUR — SAINT SELFISHNESS

1. What does the term "saint selfishness" mean?
   It is the description for saved Christians who for various reasons simply do not share Jesus.

2. According to the Bible, what was Jesus' agenda here on earth?
   Jesus' agenda was to seek and save.

3. Why are churches so reluctant to change methods of reaching people.
   Churches are reluctant to change because of their sin of selfishness.

4. What is meant by "breaking the huddle?"
   "Breaking the huddle" means that the church must leave her comfort zone of simply gathering together and go outside the church to reach lost people.

5. What is meant by a "mission diet?"
   A "mission diet" means committing to help someone else on a regular basis.

Fill in the Blanks

1. _____ is the result of our fleshly nature.
   . (selfishness)

2. A larger percentage of each successive generation is not Christian because of our _____. (selfishness)

3. The church has become so _____ that it has misinterpreted John 3:16 to say that "God so loved the church" rather than "God so loved the world." (selfish)

4. The church has become so _____ that it is failing to pray for the next generation. (selfish)

5. One of the primary purposes of the church is evangelism. Saint _____ prohibits evangelism. (selfishness)

6. We don't share Jesus because we are _____. (selfish)

Helpful Dialogue

1. We want to be happy before we are holy, but God calls us to holiness before happiness. How do we see this misunderstanding manifested in the church today?

2. The best cure for selfishness is to give yourself away. How can this be implemented in the life of a Christian and the total life of the church.

3. Every ministry of the church should have an evangelistic component. We should examine all of our ministries to determine if there is an actualized evangelistic component. If the ministry does not have an actualized evangelistic component it should either immediately implement one, or be eliminated as a ministry of
   the church. What would be the result if the above policy statement was implemented at your church.

What Will Happen If the Problem Is Not Resolved?

1. Membership in mainline churches will continue to
   decline.

2. We will stand before the servant throne of judgment
   with the blood of the next generation on our hands.

3. The Christian church as we know it today could
   become extinct.

CHAPTER FIVE

Holy Ghost "Cinderella Syndrome"

One of the primary problems of today's church is that we treat the Holy Ghost as if He is a stepchild in the Trinity. We give lip service to our belief in the Trinity. Our doctrine speaks correctly to our belief in the co-equals of the Godhead. We sing, "Holy, Holy, Holy...God in three persons, blessed Trinity," but our behavior puts less emphasis on the person of the Holy Ghost. We honor the Father, we glorify the Son, but we theologize and debate over the person of the Holy Ghost.

Such rhetoric and behavior has caused the Holy Ghost to be underutilized in the lives of believers and the church. Consequently, believers are less than conquerors, not more than conquerors, as God has promised; and the church is left in a weaker posture, unable to fulfill all her God-given purposes. This grieves the Holy Ghost. Ephesians 4:30 tell us to grieve not the Holy Ghost of God. To do so is sin. Sin is in the house.

We see evidence of our Holy Ghost "Cinderella Syndrome" when we survey the church calendar of many of our mainline churches. More often than not, the day of Pentecost is not even listed. We list and give special attention to holidays such as Memorial Day and the Fourth of July, yet no emphasis or special attention to the day of Pentecost. We would not dare think of letting Christmas pass without honoring the birthday of the pre-existent Son, Jesus. Why is it that we don't celebrate the birthday of the pre-existent Holy Ghost? On Christmas the word became flesh and dwelt among us.

The Holy Ghost should not be treated as Cinderella.

On the day of Pentecost, the Spirit became flesh and dwelt in us. Christmas represents the incarnation of the Son. Pentecost represents the incarnation of the Holy Ghost. If we are true to our doctrinal belief in the Trinity, one is as important as the other. If we have a party for one, we ought to have a party for the other. The Holy Ghost should not be treated as Cinderella.

THE DAY OF PENTECOST

As a seminarian, I took a course in New Testament Critical Biblical Methodology. One of the final examination questions that I shall never forget asked for an explanation of why the day of Pentecost was not an historical event, and why Luke never met the Apostle Paul. I gave the answer that the professor desired, then I wrote this footnote under my answer, "I don't believe a word I just wrote." Thankfully, the professor gave me credit for my answer.

As was stated in the introduction, this book does not deal with radical theology. Most mainline churches, pastors, and believers believe in the infallible inerrant word of God. The question is not our belief; the question is our behavior. Our behavior picks and chooses and ignores scriptural truth. For various reasons many have simply ignored the spiritual truths that surround the day of Pentecost. All Christian churches should be "missionary" churches. All should be "evangelical"; all should be "Pentecostal." We have no right to pick and choose. We have no right to treat the Bible as if it were a cafeteria menu. If we pick and choose, we will miss the mark somewhere. To miss the mark is sin. Sin is in the house.

All Christian churches should be "missionary" churches.

Pentecost takes place on the fiftieth day after the resurrection. We learn from Old Testament scripture (Leviticus 23:16,17; Deuteronomy, Numbers) that it represents the feast of the harvest, or the feast of the first fruit. For the Christian believer, Christ is our first fruit.

> But every man in his own order: Christ the firstfruits; afterward they that are Christ's at his coming. (1 Corinthians 15:23)

Just as the New Covenant Passover meal (the Lord's Supper) celebrates the death of Jesus, and Easter celebrates the resurrection of Jesus, so does Pentecost celebrate the fulfillment of the promised Paraclete. The term

Paraclete is a Greek word that means "counselor, friend, advocate, and helper." The Paraclete desires to be celebrated. Pentecost celebrates the fruition of the crucifixion and resurrection.

For Christians, Christ is our Passover, and Christ is our first fruit. He is our Passover because of His death, the second death will pass us over. He is our first fruit because He arose; afterward we will arise. We can ill afford to ignore or sweep this critical truth under the carpet. To do so will leave us powerless. No Holy Ghost — no power. Little Holy Ghost—little power. Much Holy Ghost—much power. We need power to live victorious lives. We need power to be more than conquerors. We need power to witness.

We cannot effectively do Matthew 28:18,19 (the Great Commission) without Acts 2 (Holy Ghost power). The Holy Ghost is not a stepchild; the Holy Ghost is the person of God. Just as Jesus is God and God is Jesus, the Holy Ghost is God and Jesus. The Holy Ghost is not a substitute for God—the Holy Ghost is God. He, the Holy Ghost, is not a second stringer. He should start and finish the game. The Holy Ghost is the only existential God present. He is our "here and now" God.

The incarnate Jesus is no longer on earth, but the incarnate Holy Ghost is here with us and in us. He has the mandate, promise, and assignment to never depart from us. His assignment is to teach us, bring truths to our remembrance, and to comfort and counsel us. Yet we hinder His function because we treat Him like a second class citizen of the Trinity. We underutilize Him. We abuse and misuse Him. We grieve Him. We sin against Him.

A BIBLICAL ILLUSTRATION — DRUNK ON THE HOLY GHOST (ACTS 2:15)

For these are not drunken as ye suppose, seeing it is but the third hour of the day.

The day of Pentecost, the fiftieth day after the resurrection, which has been designated the birthday, or debut, of the Holy Ghost and the New Testament Church, is vividly described in the second chapter of the book of the Acts of the Apostles. It could be more correctly called the Acts of the Holy Ghost.

Jesus died on Friday, arose on Sunday morning, then tarried for forty days making post-resurrection visitations before ascending on the fortieth day. During one of His post-resurrection appearances, He visited the disciples and instructed them to go back to the infamous upper room and prayerfully wait together in one accord for the promised counselor, teacher, helper, and comforter (the Paraclete), who would never depart from them. In obedience, they did as they were instructed.

Then, on the fiftieth day after His glorious ascension, it happened. The day of Pentecost came. It was powerful. It was miraculous. It was as a sound of a rushing wind that filled the room. It was not a rushing wind, but it was as a rushing wind. Cloven tongues of fire set over the heads of believers, and they were given power to speak in other tongues that various people from all parts of the ancient world understood in their own language.

One thing is certain, the tongues (languages) that were spoken needed no interpretation. Another thing for sure is that they were acting differently. Maybe later, some began to speak in unknown tongues. We don't know. The Bible does not say. Nevertheless, they were acting differently. So differently, in fact, that some supposed that they were drunk on new wine. But the newly restored and forgiven Peter, himself filled with the Holy Ghost, reminded the people that it was too early in the morning for them to be drunk on wine.

It was nine o'clock in the morning, and in ancient days, people did not drink new wine that early in the morning. They were not drunk, as supposed. Peter's response implies that they indeed may have been drunk, but not drunk on what was supposed, for they were drunk on the Holy Ghost.

> For indeed, this is that which was spoken by the prophet Joel; And it shall come to pass in the last days, saith God, I will pour out of my Spirit upon all flesh: and your sons and your daughters shall prophesy, and your young men shall see visions, and your old men shall dream dreams: And on my servants and on my handmaidens I will pour out in those days of my Spirit; and they shall prophesy. Acts 2:16-18)

One of the reasons churches don't grow is because they are too sober. The church needs to get drunk on the Holy Ghost. The church needs to receive a few DUIs (driving under the influence). The church needs to be found guilty of some WUIs (witnessing under the influence); GUIs, (giving under the influence; and WUIs (worshiping under the influence). The Bible says to pray in the Spirit (Ephesians 6:18).

The church is operating too much in the flesh and not under the influence of the Holy Ghost.

The church is operating too much in the flesh and not under the influence of the Holy Ghost. We are to work in the Spirit and not in the flesh. To operate in the flesh is disobedience to God's word and is therefore sinful. Sin is in the house.

THE HOLY GHOST: FROM CINDERELLA TO CASPER

Regardless of the names given the Spirit of God, He is supposed to be viewed as friendly, not treated as a stepchild. One of the reasons we underutilize the Spirit of God is because of fear. Admittedly, many people have a subconscious fear of the Holy Ghost. The word "ghost" itself connotes something frightening. "Spirit" does so to a lesser extent, but still implies that it is something that is outside the realm of human control. The Spirit is, indeed, beyond being controlled by the flesh.

Flesh does not like to be controlled by the Spirit. Flesh is frightened by the unpredictability of the Spirit. However, the good news is that the Holy Ghost does not hurt. We can trust the Holy Ghost to guide us correctly. But like those filled with the Holy Ghost on the day of Pentecost, it will make you act differently. You cannot be filled with the Holy Ghost and behave the same. If you are filled with the Holy Ghost, you will act differently than you would if you were not filled.

Being filled with the Spirit allows you to act differently in controlling the flesh, rather than being out of control of self.

Being filled with the Spirit allows you to act differently in controlling the flesh, rather than being out of control of self. Acting differently from the world is good. It is good to act differently when under the pressure of peers to do something that is wrong. It is good to behave differently when those at the office party are acting carnally.

To be set apart and different requires power—power that comes from the full possession and use of the Holy Ghost. To be filled with the Holy Ghost, the believer must partake of the Holy Ghost. You cannot be filled with what you either fear or feel is not primary or significant. Therefore, both the believer and the church must eradicate the Holy Ghost "Cinderella Syndrome" and view the Holy Ghost as a friendly Helper and an equal person in the Godhead.

HOUSECLEANING SOLUTIONS
SOLUTION ONE: *Celebrate the Day of Pentecost*

Noteworthy, the historic day of Pentecost cannot be duplicated. The birthday of the indwelling incarnated Holy Ghost can no more be duplicated than the historic

Bethlehem birth of Jesus. Pentecost cannot be duplicated, but it can be celebrated.

For some churches that simply means putting the day of Pentecost on the church calendar. The fact that many mainline churches have Labor Day, Fourth of July, and Memorial Day on the church calendar and omit the day of Pentecost is an indication of the severity of the Holy Ghost "Cinderella Syndrome." The suggestion is to celebrate Pentecost the same way and manner in which we celebrate Christmas and Easter.

If we would emphasize and celebrate the Day of Pentecost the way we celebrate other Christian holidays, we would win more spiritual battles.

If we would emphasize and celebrate the day of Pentecost the way we celebrate other Christian holidays, we would win more spiritual battles. The victory is won, but the war rages on. We are in spiritual warfare. Unlike Christmas, the birthday of the Son, the day of Pentecost has no competition from the world. On Christmas we have to compete with commercialism, Santa Claus, Christmas trees, and the like. However, on the birthday of the Holy Ghost, there are no ornaments or decorations. We are virtually free from secular competition. This should give the Christian believer a tremendous added advantage in spiritual warfare. Emphasizing and celebrating Pentecost will help clean the house of the sin of grieving the Holy Ghost.

SOLUTION TWO: *At Every Level, Seek and Implement God-sized Ministry Tasks.*

Here is the question, "What are you currently doing that once the task is complete, you will know for sure that God did it?" The challenge is to discover and pursue God-sized ministry tasks that, when brought to fruition, we know we could not have done it without the help of the Holy Ghost. The opportunities are there for us to discover. It can be something as simple as a building program, overcoming a secret addiction, or participating in door-to-door evangelism.

The church I pastor discovered and pursued the ministry task of witnessing and building relationships with the unsaved husband of a saved woman of the church. This suggestion should be encouraged at every level of church participation, beginning with individual believers, various ministries, and concluding with a church-wide God-sized ministry task.

Budget planning is a great time to depend on the power of the Holy Ghost.

SOLUTION THREE: *Always Factor in the Work of the Holy Ghost in Budget Planning.*

Walking in the Spirit means having faith in God. Money proves to be a great yardstick by which to measure our faith. Jesus said:

> For where your treasurer is, there will be your heart also. (Matthew 6:21)

Budget planning is a great time to depend on the power of the Holy Ghost. The suggestion is to include the unseen power of the Holy Ghost in budget planning. Many churches plan their budget based on the actual income from the previous year. This kind of budget planning is a slap in God's face; surely the Holy Ghost is grieved. Such secular budget planning is denying the expectation of the Holy Ghost in the coming year. Walking in the Spirit means planning in the Spirit. Be sure to factor in a percentage that you expect God to do through the work of the Holy Ghost.

SOLUTION FOUR: *Teach that Being Filled with the Holy Ghost is a Christian Duty Rather than a Spiritual Gift.*

Many believers think that being filled with the Holy Ghost is a special supernatural spiritual gift given to a chosen few. Ephesians 5:17,18, speaking in the context of Christian duties, rebukes such thinking by telling us:

> Wherefore be ye not unwise, but understanding what the will of the Lord is. And be not drunk with wine, wherein is excess; but be filled with the Spirit.

It is the will of God that every believer be filled with the Holy Ghost. The scripture is saying, all believers are expected to be continuously filled. In other words, all believers should walk in the Spirit and not in the flesh. This filling is not to be considered a one-time event. We are to be continuously filled. Therefore, the theological

It is the will of God that all should be continuously filled.

debate on when we receive the Holy Ghost, whether at the time of conversion or after receiving a second blessing of being baptized by the Holy Ghost, becomes somewhat of a mute point. It is the will of God that all should be continuously filled.

Skull Practice
CHAPTER FIVE — HOLY GHOST
"CINDERELLA SYNDROME"

1. What is the meaning of the title, "Holy Ghost Cinderella Syndrome?"
   It means that we treat the third person of the Godhead (Holy Spirit) as if He is a stepchild of lesser significance than the Father and the Son.

2. Is being filled with the Holy Ghost a supernatural spiritual gift or is it a Christian duty?
   There are various supernatural spiritual gifts distributed by the Holy Ghost. However, to be filled with the Holy Ghost is a Christian duty that applies to all believers.

3. Is the day of Pentecost a historic event?
   Yes. If we believe in the infallible, inerrant word of God, we must treat it as such.

Fill in the Blanks

1. When the Day of Pentecost goes uncelebrated, often not even recognized, we see ourselves as victims of

   _____ _____ _____

   _____. (Holy Ghost "Cinderella Syndrome")

2. We honor the Father, we magnify the Son, but we theologize and debate over the person of the _____
   _____. (Holy Ghost)

3. If we glorify and magnify the _____
   _____ with the same fervor as we do the Father
   and Son, we would win more spiritual battles. (Holy
   Ghost)

4. You cannot be filled with the Holy Ghost if you are
   afraid of the _____ _____.
   (Holy Ghost)

5. The _____ _____ is a Friend, a Helper, and
   an equal Person in the Godhead. (Holy Ghost)

Helpful Dialogue

1. What are you and/or your church doing that, when the
   task is complete, you will know for sure that God did it?

2. God-sized tasks require the power of the Holy Ghost.
   Discuss some personal and some church-wide God-
   sized tasks that could be undertaken.

3. Money has proven to be a great yardstick by which
   to measure our faith. How can the power of the Holy
   Ghost play a role in personal and church budget
   planning?

What Will Happen If the Problem Is Not Resolved?

1. You will never live a victorious life.

2. You will experience more valleys than peaks in your Christian journey.

3. Your church will experience only limited growth.

4. You and your church will not experience much spiritual growth.

5. You and your church will not be able to fulfill the Great Commission.

CHAPTER SIX

Diluted Corporate Worship

Worship is one of the five primary purposes of the church. Both individual worship and collective worship is of the utmost importance. However, the focus of our concern is the sin of diluted collective worship that takes place in the house of God.

The Bible tells us we should not forsake the assembling of ourselves in God, and we should worship Him in the sanctuary. We cannot and should not use individual worship as an excuse to ignore the call and command to worship God together. In other words, there is a clear mandate from God for not only individual worship, but to participate in collective or corporate worship as commanded, admonished, described, and illustrated in the Bible.

Failure to worship, as God through His word (scripture) has told us, is a high crime of sin.

Failure to worship, as God through His word (scripture) has told us, is a high crime of sin. To worship as we want to worship and not as God commands us to worship, is diluting worship. Diluting worship is sin. There is too much diluting of biblically mandated worship in the house of God. There is sin in the house.

WHAT IS WORSHIP?

Worship at best is difficult to define. Is there a difference between praise and worship? Praise and worship are closely interrelated. However, I believe there is a difference. Praise can be a one-way communication of adoration and thanksgiving to God. Worship is a two-way communication that brings us into communion with God. God is always an active participant in worship. However, we will never enter into the act of biblically based worship until we first praise God as His word tells us to do. Praise is the key that unlocks the door to worship. My working definition of worship is that *worship is an active, biblical response to the person and work of God that brings us into a greater presence of God and the presence of God into us.*

In other words, praise and worship should drive us to seek His face, and when we find His presence, we will discover a greater sense of His presence with us and in us. I am convinced that on Sunday mornings, many believers do not enter His gates with thanksgiving and do not enter into His courts with praise; they never really worship. Some make it through the gates with thanksgiving but fall short and are found lacking in the courts with praise (Psalm 100:4). So these also never experience a sense of the presence of God.

Looking at our working definition of worship, we find several distinctives. They are: (1) an active response; (2) a biblical response; (3) the person of God; (4) the work of God; and (5) a greater presence of God.

First, worship is an active response. It is not a passive response. Collective worship begins with an active expression. Worship is not a noun. Worship is not a person, place, or thing. Worship is something we do.

The scripture gives us unquestion- ably clear and definitive illustrations of biblical responses. When the church fails to respond to God in a similar fashion, we have missed the mark.

Second, worship is a biblical response. A study of Old and New Testament scripture reveals many forms of praise. They all involve activity, such as, extending hands, singing, lauding, blessing, shouting, uplifted hands, etc. "Two Old Testament Hebrew verbs spell out the heart of worship: *hallal* and *yadah.* These words mean praise, thank, bless or worship."[1]

"The word *'worship'* is derived from the Saxon term *'worthship'* and is used to indicate an attitude of homage. It is used in English to translate a Hebrew term in the Old Testament that means 'to bow or prostrate oneself,' and a Greek term in the New Testament that means the same but derives from a root meaning 'to kiss.'"[2]

The scripture gives us unquestionably clear and definitive illustrations of biblical responses. When the church fails to respond to God in a similar fashion, we have missed the mark. Therefore, once again there is sin in the house.

The third and fourth components of our working definition deals with the person of God and the work of God. These components concern who He is and what He has done. We are to worship God simply because He is God. We really need no other reason than the simple fact of who He is. But we also worship Him for His mighty works, beginning with creating us for His pleasure, in His image, and saving us with the promise of one day allowing us to see Him face to face and be like Him.

The fifth and final component deals with entering into His presence and seeking His face. Because of what God did in and through the coming of Christ, God is always with us. "Emmanuel" means "God with us." Because of what God did in and through the work of the Holy Ghost, God is also in us. He is with us as believers, and in us, and promises never to leave us. However, through worship we seek to find and experience a greater sense of His presence. God has promised when two or three are gathered in His name He would be in the midst (Matthew 18:20). When we truly worship, we enter into a special experiential relationship with God where He is in the midst.

WHY WORSHIP?

There are many reasons to worship, but one can usually sum it up in who He is and His mighty works. However, from a Christian's perspective, we must worship because in His word He tells us to worship Him. Most Christians lean on their own understanding, per-

> **Our worship has become diluted and, for all practical purposes, unbiblical. This is disobedience.**

ceiving themselves as worshipers. Herein lies the problem because we worship Him based on our own understanding and not based on biblical teaching or worship. Our worship has become diluted and, for all practical purposes, unbiblical. This is disobedience. This is sin.

Churches that permit diluted and unbiblical worship to continue Sunday after Sunday are in a backsliding posture. They resemble what God called in Hosea 4:16 (and described in the Introduction of this book as) a "backsliding heifer."

When we do not worship as God has told us to worship, we are not in a perfect relationship with Him. God tells us to worship Him in spirit and in truth (John 4:24). He, Himself, is spirit, and He, Himself, is truth. Many have a problem worshiping in spirit because they cannot see Him.

> The fact that we serve an unseen God is both a blessing and a stumbling block. It is a blessing in that our God cannot be contained or adequately expressed in three-dimensional form, for His is beyond containment—He is all in all. The problem is we are "sense conscious" creatures; we can quickly relate to what we see, hear, smell, or touch, but we have difficulty in focusing on things unseen; and this makes true spiritual worship a real challenge.[3]

Many want to worship Him in spirit that is defined by our will, but do not want to worship Him in truth that is defined by scripture.

Worshiping God in spirit is truly challenging. Oftentimes it causes us to lean on our own understanding and use the Spirit of God to authenticate and give authority to our own ideas. More bluntly, we often bear false witness against the Holy Ghost so that we can have our own way. But the Holy Ghost will not lie on Himself. God is Spirit, and God in Christ is also truth.

Jesus said, "I am the way, the truth, and the life." He is truth and His written word is truth. The word of truth will not lie on the spirit of truth, and the spirit does not lie on the word of God. We must measure what we feel in our spirit with what the word of God says.

Many want to worship Him in spirit that is defined by our will, but do not want to worship Him in truth that is defined by scripture. This leads to a watered-down worship—watered down to fit our thinking—watered down to match our personality and character—watered down to fit our level of comfort—watered down to blend with our culture—watered down to avoid practicing the truth that we have gained from interpreting scripture to the best of our ability.

When we do not practice what we know to be truth, we sin. Sunday after Sunday throughout this world, sin is running rampant in the house of God.

BIBLICAL FOUNDATIONS FOR WORSHIP

The Bible, for Christians, is the source for all worship experiences. The forms and practice of worship must be tested continuously by the revelation of God in the Bible.

Old Testament Examples

The first example is from the first commandment, which is found in Exodus 20:3-6. The Bible states:

> You shall have no other gods before Me. 'You shall not make for yourself a carved image, or any likeness of anything that is in heaven above, or that is in the earth beneath, or that is in the water under the earth; you shall not bow down to them nor serve them. For I, the LORD your God, am a jealous God, visiting the iniquity of the fathers on the children to the third and fourth generations of those who hate Me, but showing mercy to thousands, to those who love Me and keep My commandments.' (NKJV)

The first commandment, then, is to worship God and God alone. Our priority is stated in Exodus 34:14:

> For thou shalt worship no other god: for the LORD, whose name is Jealous, is a jealous God.

The establishment of the tabernacle in Exodus 25 is a proof that God wanted the Israelites to focus on worshiping Him; therefore, the tabernacle was established as a place for worship.

The Bible also declares in Deuteronomy 26:10:

And now, behold, I have brought the firstfruits of the land which you, O LORD, have given me. Then you shall set it before the LORD your God, and worship before the LORD your God. (NKJV)

This was instruction given to the children of Israel by Moses. "They were to acknowledge God as Creator, Protector, and Provider. Once in the Promised Land, each person was to place before God the firstfruits of the harvest and worship Him."[4]

New Testament Examples

The Gospels presuppose the forms of worship native to Palestinian Judaism in the early first century A.D. This means that the Temple still occupied an important place in primitive New Testament worship.

During the temptation of Jesus as recorded in Matthew 4:10 and Luke 4:8, Jesus demonstrated that worship belongs to God alone. "A lesson from this highly charged moment in Jesus' life leads one to realize that the foundation of all we do is worship."[5]

Jesus declared in John 4:24 that those who worship God must worship Him in spirit and truth. Connect this with Romans 12:1:

I beseech you therefore, brethren, by the mercies of God, that ye present your bodies a living sacrifice, holy, acceptable unto God, which is your reasonable service.

This shows what God wants out of the believer. God wants acceptable spiritual worship. The body is referring to the whole person. God calls on us to present ourselves to Him in an act of worship.

Three Wise Worshipers (Matthew 2:1-12)

Better known as the Three Wise Men, the Magi provide us with an excellent illustration of coming into His presence for no other reason than to worship Him. Note, unlike us, they had not had the privilege of knowing Him and experiencing His love. They came only because of who He was suppose to be. They simply came to worship Him:

> ...behold, there came wise men from the east to Jerusalem, Saying, Where is he that is born King of the Jews? for we have seen his star in the east, and are come to worship him. When Herod the king had heard these things, he was troubled, and all Jerusalem with him. (Matthew 2:1b-3)

I want to suggest that the portion of this scripture narrative that asks the question, "Where is He?" is what should motivate us to simply seek His face in worship. Further, the star represents the manifestation of God in our spiritual or physical lives that should lead us to worship Him. Like the Wise Men of old, we may have our quest to worship Him interrupted by the Herods of the world who represent the enemy of God; and the "Great Pretender" of worship, claiming he also wants to worship Him.

> And he sent them to Bethlehem, and said, Go and search diligently for the young child; and when ye

have found him, bring me word again, that I may
come and worship him also. (Matthew 2:8)

Unfortunately, the spirit of Herod has crept into our
church today. He has stolen much of the victory and joy
of worship out of the church. Many churches today have
allowed the "Great Pretender" of worship to influence
them. But those who have seen the star flashing in us saying, "Where is He?" push on to seek His face. We should
rejoice like the Wise Men with exceeding great joy, if
indeed we have seen the star.

When they saw the star, they rejoiced with exceeding great joy. (Matthew 2:10)

What is exceeding great joy? What is your personal
best interpretation of "exceeding great joy"? My interpretation is best illustrated by the participants in television game shows like "Wheel of Fortune," when the
contestant wins the big prize. In my opinion they are
rejoicing with exceeding great joy. Yet I seldom see that
display of exceeding great joy in our worship. Why?
We have diluted our worship. Let us press on with our
gifts of gold, frankincense, and myrrh that represent the
best that we have for God, and indeed present our bodies (our total self) to God, holy and acceptable, which
is our reasonable worship.

Noteworthy, the scripture declares that once the Wise
Men experienced worship, they did not return the route of
Herod (the world). They returned another way (Matthew
2:12b). It is time for the church to go another way. The
way of unbiblical diluted worship is not God's way.

Failure to worship God's way is sin.

Failure to worship God's way is sin. Yes! There is sin in the house. But the house of God can be cleansed of its failure to worship God in the way that is pleasing to Him, not to ourselves.

HOUSE CLEANING SOLUTIONS

SOLUTION ONE: *At Least Once a Year, Teach And/or Preach a Theme Revival on Biblical Praise and Worship.*

Preaching and teaching the word is a repetitive solution to all of the crucial problems of the church because the scriptures tell us that the word cleans (John 15:3). The word of God will clean us from the problem of diluted worship if we would diligently and rightly divide it.

At the beginning of my pastorate, the church I serve was selected as one of the fastest growing Sunday Schools in the country, and was featured in a book authored by Dr. Sid Smith entitled, *Ten Super Sunday Schools in the Black Community* (Broadman Press, 1986). To collect data for his book, Dr. Smith visited each church to observe all of their ministries.

When describing our worship ministry in the book, my dear friend, Dr. Smith, wrote what he intended to be an endearing compliment to my worship ministry. In summary he said, "When you visit the worship you will experience a highly intellectual, non-emotional setting."

I thank God today for Dr. Sid Smith and his family, as we have remained friends over the years. But I must confess that when I read his endearing statement describing our worship I thought, "How unbiblical!"

God used my good friend to make a powerful revelation to me. I was instantly convicted to change the unbiblical nature of our worship. I bowed my head in repentance, asking God to allow me to lead His people in biblical worship, based on my best discernment and interpretation of scripture—regardless of popularity, opinions, and culture. I followed the star, worshiped, and returned another way.

If you want to stop the snowballing illness of diluted worship, begin to apply the cleaning solution of God's word concerning praise and worship.

The first step in my new direction was to begin teaching and preaching revivals on what the Bible says about praise and worship. I declared one whole month out the year as "Hallelujah Month." During this month, every Sunday sermon was on the theme of praise and worship, entitled "What the Bible Tells Us about Praise and Worship."

People are transformed by the word of God; through the power of the pulpit. If you want to stop the snowballing illness of diluted worship, begin to apply the cleaning solution of God's word concerning praise and worship.

SOLUTION TWO: *Stop Excusing Unbiblical Corporate Diluted Worship Based on Culture, Tradition, and Personality Traits.*

Often we hear statements such as, "Worship should be culturally relevant" or "My passive personality and innate character does not permit me to praise God expressively." And, of course, there is the controversy over what has been labeled as "traditional worship" versus "contemporary worship." All these statements are excuses that are part of the dilution process that waters down biblical worship.

Is God's word so vague that we must rely on culture, personality, and tradition to determine how we carry out one of the primary mandates of the church? No! His word is not that weak and indecisive. Our problem is that we want to worship the way we like to worship, and in the way we are most comfortable worshiping, and in the way we are accustomed to worshiping, with no regard to our best discernment and interpretation of the scripture.

God calls believers to break through their comfort zones so that one can best be used by Him.

I find it interesting that there is no difference in how various cultures and races rejoice over winning the lottery or athletic events. Why then, should our rejoicing differ when it comes to rejoicing over the person of God and His might works? Without question, people possess a variety of personality traits. Some are introverted and some more extroverted. Some are more passive, even docile, and others more active, even aggressive. Some are shy, and yet others are bold. However, without question, flesh cannot be relied on to determine truth.

God calls believers to break through their comfort zones so that one can best be used by Him. I saw this illustrated during budget planning time at the church where I serve as pastor.

At Greenforest Community Baptist Church, we raise the budget strictly through tithes and offerings and yearly written commitments of firstfruit percentage giving to the tithing program called "Planned Growth in Giving." One year, when we were approaching a $3.5 million budget, our commitments were running below our projected budgeting expenses. I had always preached and taught that God is so faithful that you don't have to wait to celebrate what He says He is going to do. You can celebrate before He does it. One of my ways of celebrating is to literally run victory laps around the sanctuary. Sound foolish? Remember Joshua and the walls of Jericho!

Since our commitments were falling short of our projected expenses for the coming year, I had asked the chairman of our Deacon's Ministry to make a special appeal in an attempt to raise the level of commitments. Our chairman, who is a dear friend, has an introverted and shy personality, and a very conservative character. However, on the day he made the appeal, he stepped out of his normal personality and ran two victory laps inside the sanctuary in an act of praise and thanksgiving for what he was praying in faith that God would do.

Never, never, in my nineteen years of pastoring have I ever seen so many strongholds broken and believers set free on one Sunday! The very next Sunday, the first Sunday service offering was up by a whopping 30 per-

Our churches are in a backslidden posture because we have let culture, personalities, and society influence our understanding and behavior. Worship should not be filtered through anything except God's holy word. Any other filter produces dirtiness rather than cleanliness.

cent. God is calling believers to step out of the comfort zones of their personality and worship Him according to scripture.

Many churches today are embracing what has been tagged "traditional worship" and "contemporary worship." In general, traditional worship is what is desired by older generations, and contemporary worship is thought to be effective in reaching younger generations. These approaches to worship are being implemented with no consideration to what is biblical, according to our best discernment and interpretation.

Personally, I believe in tradition. However, we should be products of our traditions and not victims of traditions. I also believe we should be about the business of implementing changes in the church to meet the challenges of a changing society, but not at the expense of what is God's unchanging word. The issue should not be traditional versus contemporary. The issue should be, regardless of desired appetites for worship style, what indeed do we discern to be biblical?

Some claim that worship should never be about style or form. That sounds good and intelligent, but what if the Bible instructs and dictates style and form; then style and form of worship may indeed be significant. I believe the style and form of worship is described in God's word in the Book of Revelation; indicating what heaven will be like is significant.

When any form of praise is not focused solely on giving God glory, it is being misused, and that also is sinful.

Our churches are in a backslidden posture because we have let culture, personalities, and society influence our understanding and behavior. Worship should not be filtered through anything except God's holy word. Any other filter produces dirtiness rather than cleanliness.

SOLUTION THREE: *Strive to Become a Singing Church.*

Singing is a wonderful avenue of praise, and praise unlocks the door to worship. Of the various forms of praise, singing is the most user-friendly. Singing is met with the least resistance, and everybody can try to sing. God mentions singing more than he mentions any other form of praise, such as bowing, clapping, hand raising, and dancing. Singing is the easy form of praise, but just for the record, the dance is the most liberating.

Although singing and dancing are biblical forms of praise, the probability of singing being misused is lesser than the probability of the dance being misused. When any form of praise is not focused solely on giving God glory, it is being misused, and that also is sinful.

God admonishes us to sing throughout the Book of Psalms. To become a singing church is a good goal (housecleaning solution) for any church that wants to worship God according to His word.

SOLUTION FOUR: *Value the Relationship of Music to Worship.*

What we value most in our society is expressed in monetary ways. We talk about what we value and we focus on what we value. Also, what we value as a church is always expressed in our church budgets. Church budgets are reflections of church values. Music is a very valuable component of worship. God talked a lot about music when He spoke of praise and worship.

In 1 Chronicles 15:22, Chenaniah was appointed as the chief song leader and musician. Whenever God's people prepared to praise, the musicians were to lead the way.

The chief musician, David, the psalmist, expressed the value of music throughout the books of Psalm. He even calls for the instruments to be utilized (Psalm 150).

Music is the heartbeat of the very essence of who we are; therefore, music should be valued as an essential ministry of our churches. Thus, our focus and our budget should reflect music as a valued asset to worship. This does not mean that music should be overemphasized and prioritized over the preached and taught word of God. But music should not be the stepchild of the church.

Musicians should be selected with the same effort given to calling pastors and other church positions. Musicians should not be selected based solely on their skill level, but also on their spirituality and commitment to the total ministry of the church, and their demonstrated spirit-filled lives.

If we want to put back that which has been diluted from God's mandate for corporate worship, we should value music. When we value music as a meaningful component of worship we will go a long way toward cleaning some of the sin in the house.

Linking worship with our zeal for evangelism will push us forward from our backslidden posture relative to worship.

SOLUTION FIVE: *Link Worship to Evangelism.*

Praise and worship have functions. For example, there is victory in praise. Psalm 149 tells us that praise is a weapon that is given to the believer that will bind Satan in chains and fetters. An often overlooked function of biblically displayed worship is evangelism. Jesus said:

> "And I, if I be lifted up from the earth, will draw all men unto me." (John 12:32)

This extends beyond the cross to our lifting Him up in praise and worship. Rightly, many churches focus on evangelism as a primary purpose of the church, yet ignore the value of worship to the evangelistic ministry. Worship can be a very effective evangelistic tool. Linking worship with our zeal for evangelism will push us forward from our backslidden posture relative to worship.

SOLUTION SIX: *Emphasize Loving God as a Learning Process.*

Worship is an act of loving God.

As mentioned earlier in this chapter, the New Testament word for worship is linked to the word "kiss." Also, the first commandment is to love God. Worship is an act of loving God. However, we must acknowledge that loving is a learning process.

I love my wife more now than I loved her when we got married thirty-eight years ago. I love the Lord more now than I did thirty-nine years ago when I first experienced salvation.

Loving is a learning process. We learn to love. Deuteronomy 6:5-7 commands us to diligently teach our children to love God:

> And thou shalt love the LORD thy God with all thine heart, and with all thy soul, and with all thy might. And these words, which I command thee this day, shall be in thine heart: And thou shalt teach them diligently unto thy children, and shalt talk of them when thou sittest in thine house, and when thou walkest by the way, and when thou liest down, and when thou risest up.

Loving God is like wearing a chastity belt that protects us from sin.

When we worship we learn to love God more. Loving God is like wearing a chastity belt that protects us from sin. Therefore, worship is indeed a cleansing solution.

SOLUTION SEVEN: *Strive to Transform Worship from a Spectator Event to a Participatory Experience.*

There will be no spectator worship in heaven and there should not be any spectator worship on earth. I assure you that there will be no one sitting, observing, and being entertained by others worshiping in heaven. Everybody will be so glad to be there and not in hell that all will be rejoicing.

We have been misled into believing that we are to be entertained in corporate worship by the choir, the preacher, or others. Some believers even critique worship by critiquing the bulletin, the sermon, and the choir.

If we are indeed all worshiping in spirit and truth, there could be no bad notes, or wrong keys, or mistakes made. The purpose of the choir, preacher, song leader, and others is to lead us in worship, not worship for us.

Corporate worship is really God's party. We are the guests that God has invited to come to His party and we have been given the privilege of partying at His party. We are to come and present our gifts.

I beseech you therefore, brethren, by the mercies of God, that ye present your bodies a living sacrifice,

holy, acceptable unto God, which is your reasonable (worship) service. (Romans 12:1)

God is the host, we are the guests. It is the guest's responsibility to bring pleasure to the host. After all, according to
scripture, we were created for this purpose.

Thou art worthy, O Lord, to receive glory and hon-
our and power: for thou hast created all things, and
for thy pleasure they are and were created.
(Revelation 4:11)

I believe that participatory worship, and not spectator
worship, is the biblical model for worship. So we should
do all we can to reproduce this model in our corporate
worship service.

Let every thing that hath breath praise the LORD.
Praise ye the LORD. (Psalm 150:6)

SOLUTION EIGHT: *Establish Worship as a Priority for
the Church, and a Prerequisite for Leadership.*

Most churches tend to focus on one particular ministry
as their rallying point or home base. In most cases, it is
what God has given them to do well and usually is incorporated in the vision of the church. This is not all bad. For
example, at Greenforest Community Baptist Church, with
well over fifty established ministries, the teaching ministry is the focal point. We are totally unapologetic for our
emphasis on teaching and Christian education. However,
the danger in this is that other critical pivotal ministries,
such as worship, get treated as second-class citizens.

A healthy church has no second-class ministries that link to a mandated purpose of the church...

A healthy church has no second-class ministries that link to a mandated purpose of the church; worship is a mandated purpose. Therefore, the value of worship should be reflected in both budgeting, staffing, and allocation of time and facilities.

Worship should be emphasized as much as service. Oftentimes, when new believers come to Christ, we emphasis service and encourage them to discover their spiritual gifts and work in the church immediately. In many cases they are on fire and want to serve the Lord, but they burn out as fast as they fired up. The problem is that they skipped or bypassed and important step in the Christian journey. They have not learned to worship. Worship is about demonstrating our love to God and learning to love Him more and more.

Working for God before worshiping God is putting the cart before the horse. If they are taught to worship God first, they will work for God forever. They will not burn out because they will know and feel the presence of the love of God in their lives.

Worship, should definitely be a prerequisite or expectation for leadership. This should go without saying. However, I am fully aware of churches that have people serving on boards who are not regular worshipers. And when they attend, they are only spectators.

If a leader, or any person, is not an active, participating worshiper, they are not in a perfect relationship with God.

Many churches that emphasize Sunday School have Sunday School teachers and workers who come to Sunday School and do not stay for worship. This perpetuates the sin in the house. If a leader, or any person, is not an active, participating worshiper, they are not in a perfect relationship with God.

Let us worship and bow down: let us kneel before the LORD our maker. (Psalm 95:6)

SOLUTION NINE: *Teach Preparation for Worship and Practice "Think, Thank, and Praise" as Steps that Lead to Worship.*

If we are to be participants rather than spectators in worship, everybody must prepare. The leaders prepare. The pastor prayerfully prepares the sermon. The choir rehearses. It stands to reason that if we are going to actively participate, all must prepare. How do we prepare? First, by getting the right amount of rest before worship. It takes energy to be an active worshiper.

Second, by preparing our minds. Think on the goodness of God.

Know ye that the LORD he is God: it is he that hath made us, and not we ourselves. (Psalm 100:3a)

Third, we must prepare our hearts with an attitude of gratitude. We must come to church with an attitude of thanksgiving.

Enter into his gates with thanksgiving. (Psalm 100:4a)

Fourth, we should present our total selves in praise. In other words, thinking, thanking, and praising are components of preparation for worship. We can clean house by using this solution on Sunday morning and other times when we meet to worship.

SOLUTION TEN: *Strive to Make Worship Commensurate to His Worth.*

God has put a crown filled with righteous expectation over our heads, and we must strive to reach our crown.

This is an impossible task because of His worthiness. Our worship will never equal His worthiness. However, to strive to do so is a worthy goal of a believer. God has put a crown filled with righteous expectation over our heads, and we must strive to reach our crown. Therefore, we should live a tip-toe existence, always striving to connect with the crown. God has promised He will reward our efforts. God has promised that every good work begun will be brought to fruition (Philippians 1:6).

Because He is so worthy, let us press toward the mark for the prize of the high calling in Christ Jesus (Philippians 3:14). Remember, missing the mark is sin. Let us eradicate the sin in the house by striving to worship Him in accord with His worth.

Skull Practice
CHAPTER SIX — DILUTED
CORPORATE WORSHIP

1. What is diluted corporate worship?
   Diluted corporate worship is when the church collective-ly fails to worship God as described and commanded according to scriptures presented in the Holy Bible.

2. What is worship?
   Worship is an active biblical response to the person and work of God that brings us into a greater presence of God and brings the presence of God into us.

3. What are the distinctive component parts of the above definition?
   They are: (1) an active response; (2) a biblical response; (3) the person of God; (4) the work of God; and (5) a greater presence of God.

4. According to biblical word studies, is worship a noun or a verb?
   Worship is a verb. Worship is not a person, place, or thing. Worship is not a noun. Worship is something we do.

Fill in the blanks

1. _____ is one of the five primary purposes of the church. (Worship)

2. Failure to _____, as God through His word has told us, is a high crime of sin. (worship)

3. There is too much diluting of biblically mandated _____ in the church. (worship)

4. Praise is a key that unlocks the door to _____. (worship)

5. Churches that permit diluted and unbiblical _____ to continue are in a backsliding posture. (worship)

Helpful Dialogue

1. The first of the Ten Commandments listed in the Old Testament, as well as the greatest commandment according to Jesus, speak of loving God wholly. What is the relationship between the commandments and worship?

2. The Psalms and the Book of the Revelation speak a lot about praise and worship. Using these two biblical books as your guide, describe what worship should be like now and what it will be like in heaven.

3. Music is the heartbeat at the very essence of who we are. Therefore, music should be valued as an essential ministry of the church. What is the value of music to worship? How is what we value reflected in the life of

the church? Are worship and music valued in your church? How is it reflected?

What Will Happen If the Problem Is Not Resolved?

1. You will never experience the joy of entering into His presence.

2. You will be disobedient (sinful) to the purpose for which you were created (Revelation 4:11).

3. You will rob God of His glory.

4. You will never experience the power of praise.

5. You will not live a full, victorious life.

6. Your church will not grow to its full potential.

CHAPTER SEVEN

Ineffective Leadership

Church leadership represents the most sacred and untouchable problems of church growth.

Will the real sacred cow please stand up? Leadership, examine yourself. Church leadership represents the most sacred and untouchable problems of church growth. We dare not talk about it, and certainly not bring criticism to the subject. So we sweep it under the carpet, walk around it, and ignore it.

When one begins to talk with individuals about the failure of the church to grow due to poor leadership, a nerve is struck. A red flag goes up. A defense mechanism is kicked in.

In fact, evaluation of the church and her leaders is a precarious undertaking. Appraisals of the ancient church are readily accepted, but finding fault with the leadership of the contemporary church strikes too close to home for modern comfort. We dare not confront the problem, and if we do we are faced with the frustrating, seemingly impossible, dilemma of what to do about the problem. Yet ineffective leadership represents one of the most crucial problems in the area of church growth.

Effective leadership is crucial to the growth of any organization. The organizational body of the church is no different than the complexity of any organization. Leadership is the catalyst and continuing motivational force to church growth.

Today's churches suffer greatly from ineffective leadership. Notice the word "ineffective." We need effective leadership and, of course, godly leadership. Leadership has many component characteristics, but the bottom line is effectiveness. If asked whether we preferred a well-dressed, well-spoken, charismatic neurosurgeon or an effective neurosurgeon, all of us would vote for effectiveness.

Effective, godly leadership will ultimately be demonstrated through determined followship. Where there is no followship, there is no leadership. People who have claimed themselves to be leaders, or who have been claimed by others to be leaders, should take a good look over their shoulders. If there are no followers, a serious question is raised about their leadership.

This chapter deals with the problem of ineffective leadership. Because of the sacredness of church leadership and the many variables that surround leadership in general, I choose to limit this discussion to what I claim to be effective leadership. To broaden the discussion beyond effectiveness creates too much of a risk of becoming judgmental. In other words, to say that someone is not a leader because of style and form is to unfairly judge that person. Effectiveness, however, can be measured by outcome. Therefore, effectiveness is our focus and goal.

WHAT IS EFFECTIVE LEADERSHIP?

Effective leaders "major in majors." Contrarily, ineffective leaders "major in minors" and "minor in majors."

For a working definition, effective leadership can be defined as "a person who gets the right things done by the right people at the right time and place." Effective leaders get things done. The church today has a lot of talkers but not enough implementers.

Ineffective leadership often is dominated by rhetoric. Simply acting and reacting is not sufficient. Effective leaders will always spend approximately ninety percent of their time being proactive rather than reactive.

Effective leadership gets the right things done. In a previous work related to church growth entitled, *Faithful Over a Few Things: Seven Critical Church Growth Principles* (Orman Press, 1996), I assert that if leaders would implement these seven principles, God will grow His Church.

These seven church growth principles represent the right things to get done. Effective leaders get the right things done for the particular job at hand. Effective leaders "major in majors." Contrarily, ineffective leaders "major in minors" and "minor in majors."

Also, effective leadership gets the right things done by the right people. One of a leader's most challenging task is matching the right people with the right tasks and motivating them to do those tasks well. There is the issue of timing. An effective leader is one who plans carefully, uses time well, respects the value of others' time, and stays aware of the all important factor of timing. Knowing "when" is one of the most advantageous qualities of leadership.

In addition, all effective leaders are visionaries who constantly communicate, keeping the vision before the followers. Proverb 29:18 says that when there is no vision the people perish. But when there is no effective leadership the vision perishes. It is not enough to give the vision. Leadership must communicate, promote, and sell the vision. The prophet Habakkuk said,

"Write the vision, and make it plain." (Habakkuk 2:2)

Note that a vision is something that is out there in the future and has not yet been achieved. A vision is more than a purpose. A purpose may deal with a reason for existing, but a vision is to move to a place beyond where

...effective leadership is never satisfied with the status quo.

you are. Ineffective leadership often deals with purposes, but effective leadership deals with visions. Therefore, effective leadership always involves taking followers from wherever they currently are. So it stands to reason that effective leadership is never satisfied with the status quo. Church leaders who are satisfied with the status quo cannot really be visionaries. As a result, the people are perishing, the church is backsliding and missing the biblical mandate for growth, and there is sin in the house.

Much has been said and written about leadership. Qualities and characteristics of good leadership is unlimited. We have previously mentioned two qualities that are demonstrated in effective leaders; namely, they are proactive and they never satisfied with the status quo. In addition, I have observed a few other qualities that are unique to effective leadership. First, effective leaders are "crap takers." In other words, they have simply learned to take a lot of stuff and maintain a godly posture in the midst.

Effective leaders know how to roll with the punches. They have developed what Muhammed Ali called the "rope-a-dope" strategy, which in prizefighting involves covering up and protecting your head, stomach, and other vulnerable parts, and taking your licks until your opponent wears himself out beating up on you to no avail.

Second, effective leaders handle conflict "above the snake line." Snakes and other reptiles cannot exist at high altitudes. The lesson here is not to handle conflict on Satan's home court using his weapons. Handle conflict on a higher plane with God's love. Remember, you can't win a butting contest with a billy goat, or a quill shooting contest with a porcupine, or a urinating contest with a skunk. Don't get in the ditch with the enemy. In handling conflict, always give God home-court advantage by keeping the discussion and focus on the things of God. The hymn writer, C.A. Tindley, wrote, "There is a God that rules above, with hand of pow'r and heart of love, and If I am right, He'll fight my battle…" [1]

Effective leaders don't chase rumors about themselves or their family.

Effective leaders concentrate on being right according to God's word, and they let God fight their battles. Effective leaders don't chase rumors about themselves or their family. They don't make mountains out of mole hills. Effective leaders focus on being in the will of God, according to the word of God.

There are many biblical models of leadership, not withstanding the greatest example found in the servant leadership of Jesus. However, for effective leadership to occur in the church today, one thing is certain: an effective leader must be strong and courageous. The church today suffers not only from ineffective leadership, but suffers from weak, limp, timid, ineffective leadership. The biblical book of Joshua gives us much encouragement from God to be strong and courageous. In the first chapter, there are four times when God tells Joshua, and us, to "be strong and of good courage" (Joshua 1:6-7,9,18).

A BIBLICAL ILLUSTRATION

The Book of Joshua begins with Joshua's appointment to the position of leader, succeeding Moses:

> Now after the death of Moses the servant of the LORD it came to pass, that the LORD spake unto Joshua the son of Nun, Moses' minister, saying, Moses my servant is dead; now therefore arise, go over this Jordan, thou, and all this people, unto the

land which I do give to them, even to the children of Israel. Every place that the sole of your foot shall tread upon, that have I given unto you, as I said unto Moses. (Joshua 1:1-3)

Several points are noteworthy. First, Joshua has a history of being strong and courageous. Joshua, along with Caleb, was one of the spies who believed that God would give the victory and they could have conquered the land thirty-nine years before. But because of the people's doubt and unbelief, God had them to wander in the wilderness for thirty-nine years before, once again, coming face-to-face with the opportunity to enter into the promised land of Canaan.

Second, it is worth noting that Joshua had served under the tutelage of Moses. Joshua had been trained for the job.

Third, God gave the vision to Joshua to tell the people that they must leave from where they were and go farther. Again, leadership always involves going farther.

Fourth, God promises that based upon His history (past mighty works), He would be with Joshua as completely as He had been with Moses. However, the central point is that Joshua's strength and courage is directly connected to his obedience to follow the word of God exactly.

Only be thou strong and very courageous, that thou mayest observe to do according to all the law, which Moses my servant commanded thee: turn not from it to the right hand or to the left, that thou mayest prosper whithersoever thou goest. (Joshua 1:7)

The message of *Sin in the House* is to bring the church into conformity with scripture in all aspects of the life of the church. God has promised that if we do so, we prosper (grow) and are victorious. We learn much from Joshua and this biblical illustration about being strong and courageous, which is necessary for effective leadership. Based on what we have learned and what we know, what are some housecleaning solutions that may help solve the crucial problem of ineffective leadership?

HOUSE CLEANING SOLUTIONS

SOLUTION ONE: *Budget Adequately for Leadership Training.*

Matching one's spiritual gift mix with the ministry task to be done enhances the likelihood of that particular job being done.

Potential leaders are born, effective leaders are made. Therefore, training is a necessity. Interestingly, we do not deny the necessity for military training or athletic training, but we devalue the necessity for church leadership training. Again, church budgets reflect the church value systems. Appropriate amounts of money should be allocated each year for leadership training.

SOLUTION TWO: *Make Spiritual Gifts a Major Criteria for Appointing, Selecting, and Hiring Leaders.*

Although training is a necessity, God has gifted all believers with at least one special spiritual gift for the task of ministry. Matching one's spiritual gift mix with the ministry task to be done enhances the likelihood of that particular job being done. It is always helpful if leaders have the gift of ruling (leadership), teaching, nurturing (shepherding), and faith.

SOLUTION THREE: *Train Leaders to Train Leaders.*

Most leaders lead followers and never think of making leaders. Leaders are best qualified to make other leaders. Joshua was trained by Moses. Joshua never had a different vision. Many of our churches suffer in the area of leadership because often we have leaders with no continuity of vision or purpose.

Leaders should be expected to mentor potential leaders. Each church leader, including the pastor, Sunday school director, and others should be expected to duplicate themselves. Leaders should work toward the continuity of the church by training leaders who are capable of filling their positions when they are vacated.

SOLUTION FOUR: *Create and Provide Opportunity for People to Lead.*

People learn to lead by leading. Assume that every Christian is expected to be a leader in some area of ministry. In order for this to happen, the current leadership must give up control and ownership. Insecure pastors and other church leaders have a problem with this definable aspect of their ineffectiveness. Denying others the

Denying others the opportunity to lead a ministry task can be labeled "sin in the house."

opportunity to lead a ministry task can be labeled "sin in the house."

SOLUTION FIVE: *Raise the Bar for Leadership Positions.*

My work in the area of church growth is anchored in the premise that if a church grows spiritually it will grow numerically; although it may grow numerically without growing spiritually. This premise has often prompted the question, "How do you measure spiritual growth?"

The one definitive answer is in raising the standard for holding leadership positions. To be an effective leader one must be in a right relationship with God and others. If a person is not a tither, he is not in a perfect relationship with God. How then can he expect to lead?

Likewise, how can a person who is not a demonstrated active worshiper or Bible student be an effective leader? Also, if a person has unreconciled relationships with their family and other church members, he simply cannot lead where he has not been.

In most of our churches the bar has been set too low; therefore, we have not only attracted ineffective leadership, but we maintain and perpetuate ineffective leadership. Raising the standard for leadership positions will clean some of the carnality from the house in the problem areas of ineffective leadership information.

...ineffective leadership cannot continue to go unchallenged in today's churches.

SOLUTION SIX: *Establish a Format and Forum for Expected Reading and Dialogue on Selected Books on Leadership.*

Closely related to raising the standard, training and mentoring could be the establishment of some monitoring ministry, in which leaders could hold themselves accountable to each other relative to what is available in the vast area of leadership.

Many excellent books have been written on the subject. Much research has been done. Leaders and potential leaders must stay abreast of what is going on in the field, as well as maintain a certain sharpness of their previously learned leadership skills. A leadership forum or institute could well serve this purpose. Again, ineffective leadership cannot continue to go unchallenged in today's churches.

SOLUTION SEVEN: *Empower Leadership.*

Ineffective leadership is overcome through training, opportunity to lead, and empowering leaders to lead. Empowerment deals with not only training and giving leaders opportunity to lead but it also means giving leaders the freedom to make decisions and learn from their mistakes. Too often people hold leadership positions in name only. When we empower leaders we set them free to lead.

Ineffective leadership must not be allowed to gain a stronghold on the church.

Ineffective leadership must not be allowed to gain a stronghold on the church. Our only solution is to face the problem directly and transform ineffectiveness to effectiveness, thereby cleaning up the mess that has been left from the many years of tolerance, indifference, and fear. We can no longer be fearful of criticizing and examining the "sacred cow" of church leadership. Remember, God has not given us a spirit of fear, but one of love, power, and sound mind (2 Timothy 1:7).

Skull Practice
CHAPTER SEVEN — INEFFECTIVE LEADERSHIP

1. Why are leaders considered the "sacred cow" of church problems?
   Because it is nearly impossible for leaders to examine themselves, and congregations are generally too respectful, or afraid, to do so. Plus, even when the problem is challenged, it can very difficult to resolve

2. What is an effective leader?
   An effective leader can be defined as a person who gets the right things done by the right people, at the right time and place.

3. What is meant by effective leaders handling conflict "above the snake line?"
   It means that effective leaders handle conflict on a higher plane with God's love.

4. What does it mean to say that effective leaders have to develop a "rope-a-dope" strategy?
   This means that effective leaders must learn to roll with the punches, cover up with the whole armor of God, take a lot of stuff, and let their opponents wear themselves down.

Fill in the Blanks

1. _____ leadership is crucial to the growth of any organization. (Effective)

2. _____ leadership will ultimately be determined by followship. (Effective)

3. _____ can be measured by outcome. (Effectiveness)

4. _____ leaders are visionaries who constantly keep the vision before the followers. (Effective)

5. _____ leaders are never satisfied with the status quo. (Effective)

6. _____ leaders do not chase rumors about themselves or their family. (Effective)

Helpful Dialogue

1. Potential leaders are born; effective leaders are made. Therefore, training is necessary. How do spiritual gifts play into the process of preparing for effective leadership? Are there any special spiritual gifts that are absolutely necessary? Are there any other spiritual gifts that would be particularly helpful?

2. Mentoring is the process wherein a younger or less knowledgeable person learns, in a one-on-one rela-

tionship, from an older more knowledgeable and experienced person. Is there a mentoring ministry in your church? Could or would one be instituted? What do you imagine would be the result of participating in a leadership mentoring ministry.

What Will Happen If the Problem Is Not Resolved?

1. Congregations will continue to be dominated and victimized by the status quo.

2. Churches will be maintenance driven rather than ministry or mission driven.

3. Individual spiritual growth will be stifled, and numerical church growth will decline.

4. Our part in a covenant relationship with God will be unfulfilled and all potentiality will be crushed.

CHAPTER EIGHT

Unreconciled Racism

Racism is sin because it is undergirded by the premise that God made a mistake when He created a diverse humankind.

Racism is a sin. Racism is a theological heresy. Racism is sin because it is undergirded by the premise that God made a mistake when He created a diverse humankind.

Racism is sin because it is contrary to scripture, which says we are all made in the image of God, and the biblical claim that we are all born anew into the family of God.

Racism is alive in the institutionalized church. It must not be left to die a natural death. It must be killed. The church has the power to strike the lethal blow. It is not enough to change a doctrine and adopt a convention resolution. Rather, racism must be hung in public square.

In the words of Dr. Martin Luther King, Jr., "Like a boil that can never be cured as long as it is covered up, but must be opened with all its pus — flowing ugliness to the natural medicines of air and light, injustice must likewise be exposed, with all of the tension its exposing creates, to the light of human conscience and the air of national opinion before it can be cured."[1]

The church is much too silent and passive on the sin of racism.

The church is much too silent and passive on the sin of racism. The church has aggressively attacked the sins of homosexuality, pornography, and abortion, but has failed to promote a commensurate onslaught on racism. The Christian church remains in a holding pattern and backslidden posture on the sin of racism, thereby incapable of releasing the power of God to a lost and dying world. This is sin in the house. The church must release the holding brakes and move forward aggressively to eradicate this wrong. Racism is definitely in the top category among the ten crucial problems that prohibit church growth.

A BIBLICAL FOUNDATION FOR CLEANSING RACISM FROM THE CHURCH

First, we are all created by God. The scripture narrative that all Christians hold to be absolutely true states:

And God said, Let us make man in our image, after our likeness. (Genesis 1:26)

There is no mention of making one man superior to another. There is no order of hierarchy noted. From the origin of humankind, God made diversity in unity. We are all made as individually as snowflakes, with a different DNA blueprint, yet all the same, in His likeness and image. God looked at unity in diversity and diversity in unity and God "saw that it was good."

Second, we are all equal in Christ.

There is neither Jew nor Greek, there is neither bond nor free, there is neither male nor female: for ye are all one in Christ Jesus. (Galatians 3:28)

God could not have been any clearer in His word. His word is explicit and definitive. There is no class distinction, racial distinction, or gender distinction in God's family. We were made equal and born again equal in Christ.

Third, we are all birthed into the family by the same biblical principle—faith through grace.

For by grace are ye saved through faith
(Ephesians 2:8).

Also, John 1:12:

But as many as received him, to them gave he power to become the sons of God, even to them that believe on his name.

God did not discriminate in His biblical adoption principle of "as many as received him" are adopted into the family and become joint heirs to His kingdom. God is our Father, and Jesus is our elder Brother. We are family.

Fourth, we need each other to be whole. This is the biblical principle of family dependence. All of the parts (members) of the family are equal because they are equally important to the total function of the whole.

For as the body is one, and hath many members, and all the members of that one body, being many, are one body: so also is Christ. (1 Corinthians 12:12)

Racism has proven to be an instrument for Satan and all who fight against the forces of God. Racism is second only to blasphemy as the most powerful sin.

The eye cannot say to the hand, "I have no need of you." The eye needs the hand. Neither the eye nor the hand can exist independently. The same is true with each member (person and/or gift) in God's family.

The church will never be whole until the church realizes that we are one, and we need each other. Racism separates. Divided we fall. Together we stand. Because of racism, the church is in a fallen position. Racism has proven to be an instrument for Satan and all who fight against the forces of God. Racism is second only to blasphemy as the most powerful sin. Racism is from the very depths of hell. Racism is in the house. Racism must be removed from the house.

Racism is a spiritual problem. You cannot solve spiritual problems with political answers. You cannot eradicate sin with governmental solutions. Racism is a problem of the church. When the sin in the house is removed, then the church will be in position to be what God has called her to be. Racism is a carnal problem. The power of the Holy

The justification for slavery was the root of the sin of racism.

Ghost is the only thing capable of purging and cleansing the carnal roots of racism from our society.

THE ORIGIN OF RACISM IN THE (HOUSE) CHURCH

The justification for slavery was the root of the sin of racism. Man needed to make right in his mind and spirit that another group is less than he is, and therefore could be relegated to a subservient role.

The issue of slavery in America dates back to the late 1700's. However, by the time of the Civil War, there were more than four million Blacks held as slaves. The question is, where was Christianity in the midst of this struggle? Where was the church in this controversy? The answer is that the church was the nucleus of the controversy. As a matter of truth, the church was the deciding factor in the debate. To some extent, it may be fair to say that if it had not been for the church condoning slavery with twisted theology, racism would not be as well and alive as it is today. History speaks of many outstanding church leaders and great pulpiteers who were strong advocates of slavery.

"The church division helped to reshape the American church. Christianity in the South and its counterpart in the North headed in opposite directions. Important new denominations, such as the Southern Baptist Convention, which formed in the South, actually supported and endorsed the institution of slavery. Southern believers required a close, literal reading of scripture, then used those literal meanings to promote erroneous interpretations that defended slavery. Northerners, who emphasized the underlying principles of the scriptures, such as God's love for humanity, increasingly promoted social causes and an anti-slavery attitude.

At one time or another, nearly every major Protestant denomination, including Mormons who converted from Protestantism, taught that Blacks were cursed by being descendants of Cain and Ham.

"The religious world in the South, by justifying the enslavement of Black people in the United States, actually set the scene for the secular world to pass laws that protected slave owners' rights. Many Southerners believed that 'abolition and Union could not coexist and, given the two races, slavery was a positive good.' Southern church leaders and theologians began to develop a strong and systemic — though erroneous — scriptural defense of slavery."[2]

At one time or another, nearly every major Protestant denomination, including Mormons who converted from Protestantism taught that Blacks were cursed by being descendants of Cain and Ham. Although most Christian denominations have rescinded and recanted, the jury has already heard the testimony. The church missed her chance to nip sin in the bud nearly 400 years ago. But worse, the church has remained too silent on this sin issue ever since. The church was in the middle of the controversy then, and the church must now get in the middle of the fight to make good the promises and redemptive reconciliation purposes of God. The church is the only real solution. I believe God is raising up Christian men and women for the express purpose of bringing His complete plan of reconciliation to fruition. Until that time, evidence indicates that there is still sin in the house.

Evidence of the sin of racism is much deeper and bigger than segregated worship services.

EVIDENCE OF THE SIN OF RACISM IN THE (HOUSE) CHURCH

To point to the eleven o'clock Sunday morning worship service as evidence of sin in the house simply shadows the real evidence. Evidence of the sin of racism is much deeper and bigger than segregated worship services. Exchanging pulpits once a year on Race Relations Sunday will not solve this sin problem.

Allow me to examine a few more evidences of the sin of racism in the house. These evidences are not presented to condemn or judge, but simply to illustrate for the purpose of reconciliation and cleansing.

1. No apparent visual demonstration of White Christians to submit to or follow Black clergy leader-

ship. There has been an emergence of predominantly Black congregations that are led by White clergy leadership. However, the opposite is noticeably absent. There has been little notable emergence of predominantly White congregations that are being led by Black clergy leadership. As a matter of fact, in racially transitional communities where Black clergy were called to lead and possibly stabilize, the White congregation fled the church in much the same way as they fled neighborhoods when Blacks purchased homes in the community. We must realize this is more than misdirected attitudes about people of color. This is an evil spirit. This is evidence that the evil spirit of racism is alive and thriving in the heart of Christians.

Again, this is more than an attitude. This is a spirit. The problem is we have been treating it like it is an attitude that can be overcome by some Christian "love talk." The only way to successfully combat a spirit is with a stronger spirit. The Holy Ghost is the only answer. The Holy Ghost belongs exclusively to the church. The body of Christ (the Church) is the only solution to this sin in the house.

2. The consistent political alignment of conservative Christian coalition groups with legislative individuals, parties, and institutions that promote the elimination of welfare, the reversal of affirmative action, and oppose help for the oppressed. If the issue is designed to help minorities, particularly Black America, you do not have to wonder what side the conservative Christian coalition groups are on. The same as they were during slavery, the wrong side in the name of God. Nothing has changed in this arena. Cotton is no longer king as it was years ago when slavery was justified for the purpose of economic personal gain. But money is still the root of the evil. It does not matter whether we talk cotton and peanut fields or whether we talk silicon and chemical valleys.

The only way racism will be eradicated from society is when the Christian heart rises above the desire for money, power and prestige.

Racism is an instrument of power (to be discussed later), and the influence of the church is still on the side of the "haves." The only way racism will be eradicated from society is when the Christian heart rises above the desire for money, power, and prestige. This sounds impossible, but I still stand on the promise that "with God all things are possible."

3. The limited appointments of Blacks and other minorities in mainline denominational and associational offices. The social institution of sports and the subculture of the sports society has out-paced the church in appointing Black Americans to decision-making positions of authority within various sports organizations. This is further evidence that the sin of racism is flourishing in the house.

Many religious groups such as the Mormons, who converted from Protestantism, had policy based on scriptural interpretation (theology) that prevented Blacks from entering the priesthood. Mormons and other religious groups have since recanted their theological position, but

For the church to be cleansed from the depths of the sin of racism, the church must accept the ethnic presence of the biblical characters and heroes as who they were.

the evidence of their conversion has not become a demonstrated visual reality. Perhaps real repentance is needed. Again, this is a sin problem and it must be treated as any other sin problem, beginning with repentant confession, forgiveness, and concluding with deliverance and healing.

4. The emergence of hate groups that use moral values as a recruiting bait. The number one recruiting bait for hate groups that proclaim White supremacy in the name of God is moral values. They use positions on homosexuality and abortion to lure new converts into cults that have as their number one agenda White supremacy based on scriptural interpretation. The rise in the religion-based hate groups is alarming.

The problem is that the church remains silent, or at best passive, while small racist groups gain momentum using Christian precepts as an attraction. This is further evidence of sin in the house, and if it is left unchecked, will mushroom into a monster.

Hate groups are using the church to promote hate. Hate groups using what the church stands for to foster racism is evidence of the need for the church to take the responsibility to clean house.

5. The Westernization of the Bible, particularly the Old Testament, by depicting all the characters as

European in an African/Asian geographical locale. As insignificant as this may seem to some readers, this is evidence that racism exists in the church. For the church to be cleansed from the depths of the sin of racism, the church must accept the ethnic presence of the biblical characters and heroes as who they were.

The first eleven chapters of the Bible deal with world history, and that includes Black history, not just Jewish history. God had no problem with color of skin. He created it. He just didn't put any emphasis on it. Biblical characters should not have to transform into European to be celebrated and used as biblical models. The demonstrated need to do so is yet another evidence of sin in the house.

> **Based on God's word, Christians should be concerned about their children marrying non-believers and not concerned about them marrying a person from a different race.**

Biblically speaking, God never deals with color. The only time God deals with segregation is when He tells us to separate ourselves from those who do not worship to one Holy Living God. Based on God's word, Christians should be concerned about their children marrying non-believers and not concerned about them marrying a person from a different race. The conquests in the Bible deals with tribal issues, not color of skin issues.

6. The constant depiction of God as a White grandfather through the persistent imaging of His son, Jesus, as

> **The need to color God is evidence that racism exists in the house. Coloring God gives rise to misdirected theology to determine the origin of race.**

European. If the church is to eliminate the sin of racism and celebrate the diversity of the body in unity, it must realize that God is neither Black nor White. God is Spirit. The need to color God is evidence that racism exists in the house. Coloring God gives rise to misdirected theology to determine the origin of race.

Skin color is never an issue in the scripture. There are nations and tribes, but never as an issue of color. The word "nation" in Matthew 24:14 does not mean race. The Greek word there is "ethnos" from where we get the English word "ethnic." Europeans are ethnic, as other nations are ethnics. There is no pure nation. However, in Western civilization, Europeans have determined the standard that has spread to many other parts of the world. They produced for the world a blond-haired, blue-eyed image of Jesus as Savior, which is not biblical. Jesus was a Hebrew with mixed ancestry, including ancestors from Africa, who are named in the gospel of Matthew's genealogy of Jesus.

Michelangelo, during the Renaissance period, painted a picture of Jesus using his uncle as a model. This portrait of Michelangelo's uncle has become the "the model," or "the standard" by which Jesus is depicted. Although that is definitely not what the great artist intended, this model has fostered racism in the church by promoting a subtle sense of superiority among Whites and a sense of lost identity and inferiority among Blacks. God said, "No images" (Exodus 20:4). Disobedience to any portion of God's word is sin. Without question, there is sin in the house.

HOUSE CLEANING SOLUTIONS

SOLUTION ONE: *Mainline Churches and Denominations Should Include a Church-credit Course on Understanding Racism in Their Discipleship Curriculum.*

There are many well-meaning, born-again White Christians who don't understand racism. Racism is more than prejudice, bigotry, and discrimination. These adjectives describe individual attitudes and behaviors. Racism involves more than attitudes and behaviors. Racism is systemic. The following definitions might help explain. Prejudice simply means to prejudge. It usually carries a negative connotation, but one could prejudge positively. However, bigotry is the intensely negative side of prejudice. Discrimination means to express in attitude or reality differential treatment to people based on non-qualifying differences. Racism, though, is not only linked to these descriptors but is also linked to power and value systems.

> **There are many well-meaning, born-again White Christians who don't understand racism. Racism is more than prejudice, bigotry, and discrimination.**

The 1996 Book of Discipline of The United Methodist Church, in paragraph 72A, correctly defines racism as "the combination of the power to dominate by one race over the other races, and a value system which assumes that the dominant race is innately superior to the other." The church must deal with this definition if she is to cleanse herself. According to this definition, racism in the United States means White racism. This means that Black racism does not exist in the United States. However, many Blacks are prejudiced and bigoted.

It also means that although there are White bigots, there are many more well-meaning White Christians who rep-

The evil one has blinded the eyes of the church relative to her racism.

resent the church whose attitudes and actions are not bigotry, but simply because they are White they belong to the White racist system. Herein lies the need for the church to include in the Christian education curriculum a course of study on "Understanding Racism."

The evil one has blinded the eyes of the church relative to her racism. If you don't know you are guilty, you are not compelled toward repentance and healing. In order for the church to understand her role in eradicating this evil, she must understand enough about it to clean her own house. Hosea 4:6 says,

"My people are destroyed for lack of knowledge."

The church, especially the White church, is paralyzed due to lack of knowledge. However, if the church would declare war on the evil one and ask the Holy Ghost to pour out His anointing and train us to have a disciple's mind of Christ, the sin of racism could be removed from the house of God.

SOLUTION TWO: Promote a National Churchwide Campaign on Anti-Racism in the Church.

I believe that the elimination of racism in the church is high on God's priority list.

I recently served on two denominational churchwide campaigns. One was to raise money for a project. The other was to promote Sunday School growth within the state. Both campaigns were phenomenal. The money and energy spent was enormous. The church is well versed in the area of campaigning and promotion.

In a perfect world, we would expect the leadership to come from Christian coalitions. However, as mentioned earlier, current Christian coalitions have been noticeably absent and silent on the subject. I believe that the elimination of racism in the church is high on God's priority list.

We know that God is able. He has always called on us, and yes, even depended on us to be His co-laborers and ambassadors in His unfinished business. God is raising up new leadership for His purpose. Local churches should ask God to let them join His anti-racism movement in the world. The church is the instrument of this

The growing popularity of Black secular history and the absence of Black biblical history suggests that there is no biblical Black history.

great movement. Because the church is able, the sin of racism can be eradicated from the house.

SOLUTION THREE: *As a Part of the Christian Education Ministry, Offer Courses in Biblical Black History.*

Predominantly White, as well as Black, universities have found great value and benefit from Black Studies programs emphasizing courses in Black secular history. Once again, the church lags behind. The public school system has outpaced the church's Christian education ministry. The growing popularity of Black secular history and the absence of Black biblical history suggests that there is no biblical Black history.

This is the farthest thing from the truth. Skin color has never been an issue with God; the Bible never distinguishes who is of color and who is not. Since European White America is the dominant culture, however, it is assumed that nearly all the characters, including those that lived in an African/Asian geographical location, are White. This preposterous assumption promotes rather than eliminates the sin of racism from the church. Also, courses in biblical Black history are needed for dialogue and to refute the twisted theology (such as the curse of Ham), though recanted, that was once taught by Christian pastors and teachers to justify the offsprings of

racism–slavery and segregation. Attitudes are transformed by the renewing of the mind. If we are to clean
racism from the house of God, we must renew our minds.

> And be not conformed to this world: but be ye
> transformed by the renewing of your mind, that ye
> may prove what is that good, and acceptable, and
> perfect, will of God (Romans 12:2)

It is with the mind of Christ and the will of God in Christ
that we clean the sin of racism from the house of God.

SOLUTION FOUR: *Preach, and Stop Ignoring the Gospel of Liberation.*

White preachers, historically and currently, ignore,
overlook, and bypass the liberation thread of the Gospel
of Jesus Christ. Some even argue against it. God's work
of redemption is integrally woven by the gospel thread of
liberation. From the Old Testament to the New, there is a
call to set the captive free. The year of jubilee was for
God's church of the Old Testament (the *ekklesia*, the
called out), a year of emancipation and restoration.

Three commands were given to God's called out people
to follow in the year of jubilee:

(1) Return every man unto his possession (Leviticus
    25:10);

(2) Return every man unto his family" (v. 10);

(3) Ye shall not oppress one another (vv. 14, 17).

Jesus quotes the Old Testament prophet Isaiah (61:1-2)
when He proclaimed:

Racism causes a people to be bent over because of an oppressive system–and Christian pulpits remain silent.

The Spirit of the Lord is upon me, because he hath anointed me to preach the gospel to the poor; he hath sent me to heal the brokenhearted, to preach deliverance to the captives, and recovering of sight to the blind, to set at liberty them that are bruised, To preach the acceptable year of the Lord. (Luke 4:18-19)

Many White theologians and pastors have compromised this liberation gospel by spiritualizing the words of Jesus. In other words, they interpret "poor" to mean spiritually poor, or poor in spirit, thus justifying the need not to minister to the physically poor or oppressed. However, the use of the word "poor" in this text means to be "bent over." This is a physical and mental condition. Racism causes a people to be bent over because of an oppressive system—and Christian pulpits remain silent.

Notice, Jesus said He was anointed by the Spirit of the Lord to preach this liberation gospel. Many in the church do not consider one of the purposes of the anointing as dismantling systems of oppression and evil power structures. They have not seen the obvious truth that we are to affect and change nations through the enabling power and ability of the Holy Ghost. We must be able to affect the spirit or systems that control nations in order to disciple nations (Matthew 28:16-20).

Much of the world, approximately eighty to ninety percent, is under a spirit or systems of oppression, and because the truth of the anointing has not
been fully realized, the church, in a large measure,
has neither touched nor challenged these systems,
but coexisted with them. We in the church present
or interpret the gospel in such a way as to go along
with, instead of challenging, these systems in their
ungodly practices of racism, discrimination,
oppression of people, and bigotry.

The church does not have many preachers who
are brave enough and yielded enough to the Holy
Ghost to speak out against the oppressor and his
practice of controlling people. In fact, much of
the church world benefits from the way things are
and has no desire for things to change. Religion
that aids present power structures also rejects and
is intimidated by the anointing of the Spirit to
deal with oppression. Anyone who ministers at a
high level of the anointing of the Spirit and the
truth of God's Word will be labeled a "radical"
and "militant."

Jesus gave five directives in relation to the anointing that he received, which is an anointing we share
in as well, especially those who are called to
preach the good news of the kingdom of God. All
five are related to freedom and liberation.

One of the main purposes of the anointing of the
Holy Ghost is to take people from one state of

being to an opposite state of being. The anointing takes a person out of a state of bondage and brokenness to a state of liberty and wholeness; out of captivity to a state of deliverance; out of blindness to an ability to see; out of poverty to a state of well-being; out of being bruised to health and freedom.[3]

Liberation is a necessary part of God's perfect plan of reconciliation. God had completed His part of the plan when He bridged the gap that would eliminate any person from coming to Him when He died on the cross. No person has to be separated from God. God has reconciled Himself to us by the provision of the cross. Yet we have not reconciled ourselves to each other. God must be angry. God is calling White and Black Christians to be totally reconciled one with the other.

Although Blacks do not control the institutional system of racism, many Blacks, including the Black church, have become just as sinful as their White sinful brothers and sisters in Christ in their individual attitudes, prejudices, and bigotry toward other people. Black Christians need to understand that no matter how much the White system of racism has oppressed them, or no matter how White people have rejected

Although Blacks do not control the institutional system of racism, many Blacks, including the the Black church, have become just as sinful as their White sinful brothers and sisters in Christ in their attitudes...

God has provided us with something that transcends culture and race. It is called praise.

and mistreated them, God has called them into perfect reconciliation with all Christians. In other words, the sin of racism has not been waived from the judgment list because they were the oppressed. Christ has called for all things to be anew.

Christ has called us to preach an acceptable year of the Lord. This means preaching an uncompromising gospel of liberation under the anointing of the Holy Ghost. God's church will never become the unblemished bride that Christ is coming to claim as long as the ugly stain of the sin of racism is in the house.

SOLUTION FIVE: *Rediscover God's Universal Common Denominator – "The Hallelujah Factor."*

God has provided us with something that transcends culture and race. It is called praise. The premier word for praise is "hallelujah." As the church confronts the sin of racism, the church must overcome the reality that there are cultural differences and preferences. The church is in need of a common denominator; something that is biblical and has synthesizing power. Power that will unify and draw people together for one purpose and goal. Theology (man's interpretation of God's word) has polarized us, but the universal language of "hallelujah" was given to unite us.

Jack Taylor expounds on the universality of praise in his book entitled *The Hallelujah Factor*:

> The Hebrew word *hallal* forms the first part of this splendid word which I have labeled the premier word for praise. I am told that this word has transcended the language barrier among the major languages of the world. Because of the providence of God, I believe, the original word was such in majesty and completeness that instead of being translated, it was transliterated. This means that it is pronounced essentially the same as it was in the original. Thus, in English, it is pronounced hallelujah; in Italian it is pronounced hallelujah; in Spanish it is pronounced hallelujah, ad infinitum. We have in this marvelous word a combination of two Hebrew words. The first, *hallal*, means 'to boast, to brag on, to laud, to make a show, even to the point of looking foolish.' The second, *jah*, is simply the shortened name for God. Thus hallelujah became the spontaneous outcry of one excited about God, the exclamation of one upon whose consciousness part of the majesty of God has dawned. I remind you that word *hallal*, from which hallelujah is derived, is found ninety-nine times in the Old Testament. The word hallelujah is used only twenty-four times, all of them in the Psalms and occurring between Psalm 104 and 150. The distinction, I believe, is worthy of note.[4]

Praise as a universal language, practiced in obedience, will help eradicate the sin of racism from God's church.

In order to dismantle the evil of racism in the church, we must learn to celebrate our diversity and not fear our differences.

Racism is evil. Among the many virtues of praise is the biblical truth that God provided it as a weapon for the church to bind up wickedness. Psalm 149:6-9 declares:

> Let the high praises of God be in their mouth, and a two-edged sword in their hand; To execute vengeance upon the heathen, and punishments upon the people; To bind their kings with chains, and their nobles with fetters of iron; To execute upon them the judgment written: this honour have all his saints. Praise ye the LORD.

Praise is not only a common denominator, it is also a weapon. If the church is going to break the chains of the bondage of sin of racism, an aggressive offensive strategy is needed. The hallelujah factor must be a part of this fight to clean the house of this evil.

SOLUTION SIX: *Organize, Promote, and Implement an Anti-Racism Community-wide Communion Worship Service.*

In order to dismantle the evil of racism in the church, we must learn to celebrate our diversity and not fear our differences. Ignorance manufactures fear. One of the reasons we are fearful is because we are ignorant relative to know-

What better way to satisfy this purpose of the church than through the love feast?

...our goal is not necessarily to become a multi-cultural church, rather our goal is to clean the evil of racism from the house of God.

ing each other. Our fears have caused us to fail the biblical mandate of fellowship. Ignorance and fear have caused us to reduce the *koinonia* to our 11 o'clock handshaking, holy kisses and hugs, and an occasional fellowship meal. When people of different races fulfill the church's *koinonia,* they will discover that they are more similar than dissimilar. Our similarities far outweigh our differences.

What better way to satisfy this purpose of the church than through the love feast? The early church did it from house to house. We should at least be able to do it from church to church— crossing racial, cultural, and denominational lines. The celebration of the Lord's Supper/Holy Communion is an excellent way to combat racism. God called us to be in love and charity before we partake of this feast. This feast is a love feast of remembrance. Ignorance manufactures fear, but perfect love casts out all fear. The communion service should have one united focus, that is, the table and all it represents. Historically and currently, the Lord's Table is highly reverenced by all races and cultures.

Pray about starting a regular Anti-racism Community-wide Church Communion Service in your area. Notice, we call this service an anti-racism service and not the usual soft title of a multi-cultural worship service. The reason is that our goal is not necessarily to become a multi-cultural church; rather our goal is to clean the evil of racism from the house of God.

Skull Practice
CHAPTER EIGHT — UNRECONCILED RACISM

1. Why is racism sin?
   Racism is sin because it is contrary to scripture that says we are all made in the image of God, and the biblical claim that we are all born anew in Christ.

2. What evidence, other than the Sunday morning segregated worship services, exists that reveals that racism is still a problem for the church?
   Several are listed below:
* *No apparent visual demonstration of White Christians to submit to follow Black clergy leadership.*
* *The consistent political alignment of conservative Christian coalition groups with legislative individuals, parties, and institutions that oppose anti-poverty measures, elimination of welfare, and oppose help for the oppressed.*
* *The limited appointment of Blacks and other minorities in mainline denominational and regional or district offices.*
* *The emergence of hate groups that use moral values as recruiting bait.*
* *The Westernization of the Bible; particularly the Old Testament, by depicting all the characters as European in an African/Asian geographical locale.*

- *The depiction of God as a White grandfather through the persistent imaging of His son, Jesus, as European.*

3. What is racism?
   The combination of the power by one race to dominate over other races, and the value system which assumes that the dominate race is innately superior to the others.

Fill in the Blanks

1. _____ is sin. (Racism)

2. _____ is alive in the institutionalized church. (Racism)

3. In America, the justification for slavery was the root of the sin of _____. (racism)

4. _____ is a spiritual problem. (Racism)

5. _____ is a carnal problem. (Racism)

Helpful Dialogue

1. Historically, the church was the nucleus of the slavery controversy that fueled the sin of racism in America. How has the church perpetuated racism though its action or inaction?

2. Racism involves more than attitudes and behaviors. Racism is systemic. Discuss the differences and the rela-

tionships between terms such as prejudice, bigotry, discrimination, and racism. If everyone understood these differences, do you think it would help the problem?

3. Predominately White, as well as Black, universities have found great value and benefit from Black studies programs emphasizing courses in Black secular history. The growing popularity of Black secular history, and the absence of Black biblical history, suggests that there is no biblical Black history. This is the farthest thing from the truth. What do you think the outcomes would be if both White and Black churches include a course in Biblical Black History in their Christian education curriculum?

What Will Happen If the Problem Is Not Resolved?

1. The church will continue to be a partner in a theological heresy.

2. God's plan of reconciliation will not be fulfilled on earth.

3. The world will continue to make mockery of the church.

4. The church will never effectively reach a lost world.

5. Rape, murder, theft, and other crimes will continue to run rampant.

6. The church will never be whole.

CHAPTER NINE

Mishandling the Accursed/Devoted Things of God: *Stealing God's Glory*

Sin creeps into the house when we are disobedient and take God's devoted things for ourselves.

The reason why many churches are not blessed with growth is because they have mishandled the "accursed" or "devoted" things of God. The King James authorized version refers to them as accursed, while most modern translations refer to the things as devoted things. What are they? They are the "sacred things" of God. They are the things that are holy unto the Lord. Devoted things are things that belong to the Lord and are set aside for the Lord alone.

Sin creeps into the house when we are disobedient and take God's devoted things for ourselves. In the Old Testament, when God's people overcame the stronghold of

Jericho, they were instructed not to keep any of the accursed/devoted things for themselves unless they become cursed and utterly destroyed:

> And ye, in any wise keep yourselves from the accursed thing, lest ye make yourselves accursed, when ye take of the accursed thing, and make the camp of Israel a curse, and trouble it. (Joshua 6:18)

According to the law there was a "ban" that prevented the Israelites from taking any of the spoils in victory from certain Canaanite cities:

> And thou shalt gather all the spoil of it into the midst of the street thereof, and shalt burn with fire the city, and all the spoil thereof every whit, for the LORD thy God: and it shall be an heap for ever; it shall not be built again.

> And there shall cleave nought of the cursed thing to thine hand: that the LORD may turn from the fierceness of his anger, and shew thee mercy, and have compassion upon thee, and multiply thee, as he hath sworn unto thy fathers. (Deuteronomy 13:16-17)

This was purposed because of the evil practices and idiolatry of the Canaanite people. The Canaanites represented a stronghold of rebellion against God. Apparently, however, the gold, silver, bronze and other articles of iron were to be kept and dedicated to God in the tabernacle and in service to the Lord. These articles were also considered to be devoted things. None of these articles could be kept for self. All the devoted things had to be given entirely to God. Some of the devoted things were totally destroyed, other devoted articles were dedicated to God, but none were to be kept for self.

An Old Testament Example

Joshua 7 records the defeat at the City of Ai because of the sin in the camp of the Israelites that resulted from Achan stealing some of the accursed/devoted things. Joshua and the people of God had overcome the stronghold of mighty Jericho by the providential hand and promise of God. They were given the promise of victory based on their obedience in carrying out instructions to engage in a praise, faith march around the city.

The next city to be conquered was Ai. Rather than waiting on God's instruction, however, Joshua leaned on his own understanding and sent out a limited number of soldiers to capture Ai. The army of Ai defeated the Israelites and Joshua was distraught. How could God let little Ai defeat them after giving them victory over big Jericho?

Several reasons seem apparent. First, Joshua was guilty of the sin of overconfidence. Second, Joshua was guilty of not consulting the Lord before acting on his own. According to God, however, the reason for the defeat was because of the sin in the camp that resulted from somebody stealing some of the accursed/devoted things.

> And the LORD said unto Joshua, Get thee up; wherefore liest thou thus upon thy face? Israel hath sinned, and they have also transgressed my covenant which I commanded them: for they have even taken of the accursed thing, and have also stolen, and dissembled also, and they have put it even among their own stuff. (Joshua 7:10,11)

It was revealed that Achan had taken for himself some of the accursed/devoted things and hid them in the ground in his tent. For his sin, Achan and his whole family were stoned to death and burned to cleanse the camp of this sin.

Using the heart, mind, and life of Jesus as the nucleus of all scripture interpretation, I do not believe that God would have us stoning to death or burning church members as a method of eradicating sin from the house. However, I do believe the scripture reveals to us how God feels about sin in the house. He wants it eliminated. Sin in the house must be treated ruthlessly. Sin in the house must be cleansed intentionally and intensely. God hates sin and particularly when it is found in His own residence.

Sin in the house must be cleansed intentionally and intensely. God hates sin and particularly when it is found in His own residence.

SPECIFIC ACCURSED/DEVOTED THINGS

What are some of the accursed/devoted things that concern God? There are a few that the scriptures intentionally address. For example, the tithe could be labeled an accursed/devoted thing. The book of Leviticus speaks of the tithe as devoted:

Notwithstanding no devoted thing, that a man shall devote unto the LORD of all that he hath, both of man and beast, and of the field of his possession, shall be sold or redeemed: every devoted thing is most holy unto the LORD. None devoted, which shall be devoted of men, shall be redeemed; but shall surely be put to death. And all the tithe of the land, whether of the seed of the land, or of the fruit of the tree, is the LORD's: it is holy unto the LORD (Leviticus 27:28-30).

The tithe is holy unto God. What does "holy unto God" mean? Are there things that are holy unto us? Nearly forty years of marriage has taught me that my time with my wife is holy unto her. To some of us, leisure time activities appear to be holy unto us. To an avid fisherman, tennis player, or golfer, their sport is holy unto them. To some, shopping is holy unto them. What is holy unto one receives a devoted amount of one's time, energy and thought. One does not want to give up or lose what is holy unto them. God does not want to give up His tithe.

The tithe is holy unto the Lord and is, therefore, an accursed/devoted thing. Malachi declares that because we have robbed God of His tithe:

> Ye are cursed with a curse: for ye have robbed me, even this whole nation. (Malachi 3:9)

"Cursed giving" is discussed in another chapter in detail, however, noteworthy is the spiritual truth that the tithe is so important to God that we can categorize it as accursed and devoted. Mishandling the accursed/devoted tithe is a major problem relative to sin in the house.

Another mishandled accursed/devoted thing of God's that stifles spiritual and numerical church growth is the treatment and disrespect of God's pastors. Pastors are devoted things of God. A popular gospel talk show in Atlanta devoted an entire evening to what was entitled "Clergy Killers." The dialogue centered around a number of church members, who I surmise, see their existence for being in the church is to keep the pastor in place. They see themselves as watchdogs. They are clergy killers. They undermine the pastor intentionally and purposefully. They do it in the name of God and His purpose. They allow themselves to be used as instruments of Satan. They are confused. They think the pastor should be the underdog rather than the under-shepherd. On two occasions in scripture, God tells us specifically:

...in many mainline churches, pastors have been relegated to a subservient role, or at best an employee. If the pastor is an employee, then, in effect, he is owned by the church.

… touch not mine anointed, and do my prophets no harm (1 Chronicles 16:22 and Psalm 105:15).

Yet, in many mainline churches, pastors have been relegated to a sub-servient role, or at best an employee. If the pastor is an employee, then, in effect. he is owned by the church. He is the church's employee.

The root of mishandling the accursed/devoted things is ownership, which happens to be a sin as old as the problem of Adam and Eve in the Garden of Eden. They wanted to own God's garden. The Garden of Eden was an

God's plan for His church is to be led by anointed leadership.

accursed/devoted thing. Likewise, God's pastor is a devoted thing of God and should not be owned and jerked around by well-meaning, but unscriptural church boards. God's plan for His church is to be led by anointed leadership. The Apostle Paul, in his great dissertation to the churches at Corinth and Ephesus quotes:

> For the scripture saith, Thou shalt not muzzle the ox that treadeth out the corn. And, The labourer is worthy of his reward. (1 Timothy 5:18)

And God's law in Deuteronomy 25:4:

> Thou shalt not muzzle the ox when he treadeth out the corn, in an attempt to teach us this lesson: For it is written in the law of Moses, Thou shalt not muzzle the mouth of the ox that treadeth out the corn. Doth God take care for oxen. (1 Corinthians 9:9)

Paul is justifying the right of ministerial support not only for wages but also the right to lead. A major cause of church stagnation is that the church has the right away from the pastor or overseer to lead. This is an accursed act of ownership that has caused the church to be cursed. Paul tries to make this spiritual truth clear by quoting the prophet Isaiah (51:7) to the New Testament church at Rome, and us:

> And how shall they preach, except they be sent? as it is written, How beautiful are the feet of them that

preach the gospel of peace, and bring glad tidings of good things. (Romans 10:15)

The sin of mishandling God's pastor has crippled the church. Accursed/devoted things should be handled according to God's devoted word. Claiming and owning what God has devoted to Himself is a very prevalent sin in the house that needs to be utterly destroyed.

Essentially, this whole book is about the mishandling of God's church, which is certainly a devoted thing. The absolute certain reason why churches don't grow is because we want to own and control God's church. The church belongs to God, not us. He paid for it with the blood of His Son. Yet, our behavior indicates that we think we own the church. In principle, if the leadership of the church will give up control, and the membership will give up ownership, God will grow His church. God's church is an absolute devoted thing of God.

To steal God's glory is one of the most abominable sins that exists in God's house today.

GOD'S PASSIONATE ACCURSED/DEVOTED THING: HIS GLORY

Yes, the tithe, God's anointed spokesperson, and God's church are all devoted/accursed things. But throughout all time, God has been passionate about His glory. God's glory is God's passionate accursed/devoted thing. To steal God's glory is one of the most abominable sins that exists in God's house today. Our problem is too much man and too little God. Our behavior indicates that we have been affected by the philosophy of humanism. Humanism is the belief that there is some good and power in humans, that is separate and apart from God. The biblical truth we must adhere to is that there is nothing apart or separate from God. *Soli Deo Gloria* — to God alone be the glory.

Notice, in the springboard scripture concerning accursed/devoted things, when Joshua asked Achan to confess his sin of stealing the accursed/devoted things, Joshua told him to give God the glory.

> And Joshua said unto Achan, My son, give, I pray thee, glory to the LORD God of Israel, and make confession unto him; and tell me now what thou hast done; hide it not from me. (Joshua 7:19)

Achan was stoned and burned for not giving God the glory. God has always been passionate about His glory.

Nebuchadnezzar was changed to a beast for not giving God the glory.

> The same hour was the thing fulfilled upon Nebuchadnezzar: and he was driven from men, and did eat grass as oxen, and his body was wet with the dew of heaven, till his hairs were grown like eagles' feathers, and his nails like birds' claws. And at the end of the days I Nebuchadnezzar lifted up mine eyes unto heaven, and mine understanding returned unto me, and I blessed the most High, and I praised and honoured him that liveth for ever, whose dominion is an everlasting dominion, and

his kingdom is from generation to generation. (Daniel 4:33-34)

The church is currently walking in an explosive minefield as it relates to taking God's accursed/ devoted thing called glory.

Herod was smitten by an angel for not giving God the glory:

And upon a set day Herod, arrayed in royal apparel, sat upon his throne, and made an oration unto them. And the people gave a shout, saying, It is the voice of a god, and not of a man. And immediately the angel of the Lord smote him, because he gave not God the glory: and he was eaten of worms, and gave up the ghost. (Acts 12:21-23)

The church is currently walking in an explosive minefield as it relates to taking God's accursed/devoted thing called glory. We must dispose of the mines and clear a path of safety so God can grow His church and draw people to His praise and glory.

A LESSON FROM THE PROPHET JEREMIAH

Thus saith the LORD, Let not the wise man glory in his wisdom, neither let the mighty man glory in his might, let not the rich man glory in his riches: But let him that glorieth glory in this, that he understandeth and knoweth me, that I am the LORD which exercise lovingkindness, judgment, and

righteousness, in the earth: for in these things I
delight, saith the LORD. (Jeremiah 9:23-24)

Jeremiah prophesied largely to the Southern Kingdom
before they were marched off into exile in Babylon for 70
long years because of their sins. In an attempt to prevent
this from happening, Jeremiah warned the people not to
steal God's glory relative to wisdom, strength, or riches.
The lesson and warning is applicable for the church
today. The church, and the people of God for the 21st
Century, can ill afford to think or act like wisdom comes
from man. Our church facilities, budgets, ministries, etc.
all come from God, and He alone must receive the glory.

The lesson teaches us three basic spiritual truths. First,
the knowledge of God is the only real glory of man. God
is such a loving God that He connects our understanding
with His delight.

But let him that glorieth glory in this, that he
understandeth and knoweth me, that I am the LORD
which exercise lovingkindness, judgment, and
righteousness, in the earth: for in these things I
delight, saith the LORD. (Jeremiah 9:24)

Second, we learn that our possessions (riches) should
be our servant, not our masters. The expressions "a self-
made man" or "pulling yourself up by your own boot-
straps," are contrary to the will of God. Many a Christian
has fallen victim to riches. God not only permits riches
and prosperity, but it is He who gives riches and prosperity. However, when our wealth and strength become our

master and not our servant, we have crossed the line and stolen an accursed/devoted thing of God.

Third, we learn that stealing God's accursed/devoted thing of glory can lead to personal and community destruction. Moses was not permitted to immediately enter the Promised Land because he took some of God's glory:

> Take the rod, and gather thou the assembly together, thou, and Aaron thy brother, and speak ye unto the rock before their eyes; and it shall give forth his water, and thou shalt bring forth to them water out of the rock: so thou shalt give the congregation and their beasts drink. And Moses took the rod from before the LORD, as he commanded him. And Moses and Aaron gathered the congregation together before the rock, and he said unto them, Hear now, ye rebels; must we fetch you water out of this rock? And Moses lifted up his hand, and with his rod he smote the rock twice: and the water came out abundantly, and the congregation drank, and their beasts also. And the LORD spake unto Moses and Aaron, Because ye believed me not, to sanctify me in the eyes of the children of Israel, therefore ye shall not bring this congregation into the land which I have given them. (Numbers 20:8-12)

Like Moses, Achan, Herod Agrippa, Nebuchadezzar, and others, the nation of Judah fell to destruction because they took an accursed/devoted thing—God's glory.

A Lesson from the Apostle Paul

It is not expedient for me doubtless to glory. I will come to visions and revelations of the Lord. I knew a man in Christ above fourteen years ago, (whether in the body, I cannot tell; or whether out of the body, I cannot tell: God knoweth;) such an one caught up to the third heaven. And I knew such a man, (whether in the body, or out of the body, I cannot tell: God knoweth;) How that he was caught up into paradise, and heard unspeakable words, which it is not lawful for a man to utter. Of such an one will I glory: yet of myself I will not glory, but in mine infirmities. For though I would desire to glory, I shall not be a fool; for I will say the truth: but now I forbear, lest any man should think of me above that which he seeth me to be, or that he heareth of me. And lest I should be exalted above measure through the abundance of the revelations, there was given to me a thorn in the flesh, the messenger of Satan to buffet me, lest I should be exalted above measure. For this thing I besought the Lord thrice, that it might depart from me. And he said unto me, My grace is sufficient for thee: for my strength is made perfect in weakness. Most gladly therefore will I rather glory in my infirmities, that the power of Christ may rest upon me. (2 Corinthians 12:1-9)

To "glory" means to boast or brag. The apostle Paul had been blessed with special revelations directly from God Himself. Paul was caught up in a paradise, or a third heaven, where he personally experienced God. This put Paul in a special category among men. There was a temptation to boast or glory in these revelations and encounters with God. Paul felt that he should not boast on himself. As a matter of fact, it would have been foolish to boast on himself. He could, however, boast on God without bending any truth.

But to make sure that the would not fall victim to the sin of stealing God's accursed/devoted glory, God gave him a reminder (a thorn in the side) to keep him ever mindful that God alone should get the glory. Much speculation has gone forth relative to exactly what Paul's thorn really was. Paul never tells what his thorn was. Neither shall I reveal my personal thorn. However, I, like Paul, have been given a thorn in the flesh to remind me that when men applaud my achievements and good works, it is God who must receive the glory. Oftentimes, in a fleshly moment of weakness, when I am getting a "big head" (inflated ego), God will twist my thorn and the pain will help me "come to myself" and realize that it is God and not I who should get the glory.

Pastors, church leaders, and all believers today can benefit from having a thorn in the side.

Pastors, church leaders, and all believers today can benefit from having a thorn in the side. If we don't have a special thorn, like Paul, myself, and others, then realize that "we all have fallen short of His glory, and that we are saved by grace through faith less any person should boast." Paul besought the Lord three times to remove the painful thorn, but rather than removing the thorn, God reminded Paul that grace was sufficient to bear the pain. The same all-sufficient grace is responsible for our salvation.

> "Sinning is a 'falling short' of the glory of God. But the Greek word for "falling short" *(husterountai)* means "lack." The idea is not that you shot an arrow at God's glory and the arrow fell short, but that you could have had it as a treasure, but you don't. You have chosen something else instead. This is confirmed in Romans 1:23 where people "exchanged the glory of the incorruptible God for an image." That is the deepest problem with sin: it is a suicidal exchange of infinite value and beauty for some fleeting, inferior substitute. This is the great insult."[1]

Paul concludes our New Testament lesson by telling us that when he is weak, then he is strong. This supports our lesson from the prophet Jeremiah that teaches us not to glory in strength, for our strength comes from the Lord. Infirmities, handicaps, disabilities, and weaknesses tend to make us rely on God. Therefore, if we should boast, we, like Paul, should boast in our weakness so that we will not be found guilty of taking any of God's accursed/devoted glory.

A THEOLOGY OF GOD'S PASSION FOR HIS GLORY

According to the catechism, the chief aim of man is to glorify God and enjoy Him forever. Interestingly, this aim links His glory with our joy. According to Piper in a book entitled, *God's Passion for His Glory*, "God's aim in creating the world was to display the value of His own glory, and that this aim is no other than the endless, ever-increasing joy of His people in that glory. Thus, the exhibition of God's glory and the deepest joy of the human soul are one thing. God's passion for His own glory and His passion for my own joy in Him are not at odds.

God's righteousness is not the enemy of His mercy."[2] What a revelation! God, in His goodness, has allowed us to rejoice, yes, even enjoy His prized accursed/devoted thing. This implies that everything we do must be done to His glory with enjoyment. We, therefore, find everlasting joy singing to His glory, preaching to His glory, witnessing to His glory and everything we do in His glorious name. This means that although worship is God's party, He allows us to party hearty (have a good time) at His party.

...although worship is God's party, He allows us to party hearty (have a good time) at His party.

The failure of the church, and believers, to find rest, peace, and joy in His glory is sin in the house. Our churches are sick and sad because we have stolen the glory from Him. In essence, we make ourselves sick by stealing His glory. We rob ourselves of His will for our joy by taking His accursed/devoted glory. The church is in a sad state of affairs. Too much man and too little God has put us in a backslidden and immobilized position. The

Competition between local churches is the root of the evil that eventually leads to us taking the credit for what God has done.

church needs some balm from Gilead. The good news is that it is available in His glory. Giving Him glory is a house cleansing solution.

HOUSE CLEANSING SOLUTIONS

SOLUTION ONE: *When possible, avoid comparisons.*

When pastors and church members talk shop, the conversation usually leads to comparing numbers relative to church size, Sunday School attendance, sanctuary capacity, etc. As well meaning and natural as these conversations tend to flow, it robs God of an accursed/devoted thing: His glory.

Comparisons tend to focus on us rather than on what God has done. Comparison is the springboard for competition. Competition between local churches is the root of the evil that eventually leads to us taking the credit for what God has done. Church leaders and congregations should, when at all possible, avoid comparison conversations, just as Christians should avoid gossip. Realistically, oftentimes it is impossible to avoid the attention given man for what God has done.

When these times arise, make sure you, your constituents, and audiences know by your strong articulation that "God did it." Paul said:

yet not I, but Christ liveth in me. (Galatians 2:20)

...many mainline churches don't create enough opportunities, or create a comfortable and safe environment for her members to express testimonies to the glory of God. Seldom is there enough time allotted in the regular Sunday morning service.

SOLUTION TWO: *Provide Great Opportunities for Testimonies.*

In many churches, the only time set aside for testimonies is when there is an attempt to raise money or to do campaign promotions of one sort or another.

According to our theology of stealing God's glory, this in itself becomes questionable as to whether or not we are stealing an accursed/devoted thing of God's. God loves testimonies. God can always use a testimony to His glory. But we should make sure that they are given for His glory.

The problem is that many mainline churches don't create enough opportunities, or create a comfortable and safe environment for her members to express testimonies to the glory of God. Seldom is there enough time allotted in the regular Sunday morning service.

Therefore, special testimony services and other opportunities must be provided to teach and encourage the body of Christ to express that "God did it." Testimonies as a regular discipline of Christian behavior will help us not to mishandle God's accursed/devoted thing—His glory.

SOLUTION THREE: *Teach God-esteem Rather Than Self-esteem.*

Self-esteem may be described as a popular commodity. Because of the need and demand for self-esteem, it is being marketed in the form of lectures, workshops, motivational kits, videos, books and other publication. Without question, the need is plentiful. Adults and especially youth are found wanting and void in the area of self-esteem. The problem is that self-esteem is not found in self. Self-esteem is found in God. We are to love God first, then others as we love ourselves. If we do not love God first, we will never love ourselves according to God's will.

Self-esteem without God-esteem is sinful. Self-esteem without God-esteem robs God of His accursed/ devoted glory.

Self-esteem without God-esteem is sinful. Self-esteem without God-esteem robs God of His accursed/devoted glory. Christians need to be careful as they attempt to minister to the needs of the whole person, and try to meet the needs of the community. God-esteem must precede self-esteem if we are to rid the church of the problem of mishandling God's accursed/devoted things.

SOLUTION FOUR: *Practice Expressive Praise in Individual and Collective Worship.*

Notice, the term "practice" is used. This is intended to convey that no dialogue or theological debate is advised relative to what is real true praise and/or its relationship to authentic worship. The suggestion is to practice praise according to how it is revealed in scripture.

Pride and praise are incompatible. Pride is the number one adversary of God's glory.

Pride and praise are incompatible. Pride is the number one adversary of God's glory. Praise, according to Psalm 149, is a weapon given to believers to combat evil.

Let the high praises of God be in their mouth, and a two-edged sword in their hand; To execute vengeance upon the heathen, and punishments upon the people; To bind their kings with chains, and their nobles with fetters of iron. (Psalm 149:6-9)

Pride is evil. According to Proverbs, it is the first of the most hated sins.

These six things doth the LORD hate: yea, seven are an abomination unto him: A proud look, a lying tongue, and hands that shed innocent blood, An heart that deviseth wicked imaginations, feet that be swift in running to mischief, A false witness that speaketh lies, and he that soweth discord among brethren. (Proverbs 6:16-19)

Pride stands in the pathway of God's glory. Pride often dominates a believer's personhood. Therefore, practice praise and bind and chase the devil out. Theologically speaking, based on Psalm 149:6-9, one can literally praise the hell out of oneself. The church has stolen God's accursed/ devoted thing—His praise. The remedy—

Praise the Hell out of the Church. For additional information on this solution see the author's book entitled, *Praising the Hell Out of Yourself* (Orman Press, 1999).

SOLUTION FIVE: *Prioritize Worship Before Work.*

Too often, new converts are immediately thrown into the church job market without first learning to love God. This is the number one cause of "believer burn-out." Believers burn out in service for the Lord.

Without question, God is glorified in our service. However, worship is the source of our supply for service. The greatest commandment is to:

> Love the Lord thy God with all thy heart, and with all thy soul, and with all thy mind. This is the first and great commandment. (Matthew 22:37-38)

...to try to serve God without first learning to love God (worship) is putting the wagon before the horse.

The assumption is made that we can learn to love more. Our love for God can grow. I love God more today than I loved Him at the time of my conversion. Worship teaches us and helps us grow in our love for God. Believers do not suffer from worship burn-out, they suffer from service burn-out.

If we love God, we will serve God. However, to try to serve God without first learning to love God (worship) is putting the cart before the horse. Both worship and service glorify God. But prioritizing worship before service assures the continuation of His glorification.

SOLUTION SIX: *Commemorate Pivotal Blessed Events in the Life of the Church with Permanent Visual Dedications.*

In the Old Testament, when God blessed in a special way, the Israelites built an altar to commemorate the blessed event.

> Then Joshua built an altar unto the LORD God of Israel in mount Ebal (Joshua 8:30).

For God to bless the church, and the blessing not to be memorialized, is as sinful as Achan hiding God's accursed/ devoted things in his tent under the ground.

In society, we build monuments like the most recent wall in Washington commemorating the Viet Nam War heroes; or the wall in Montgomery, Alabama commemorating the slain civil rights heroes. To assure that God will get the glory, we should erect something just as Joshua did in Joshua 4:6:

> That this may be a sign among you, that when your children ask their fathers in time to come, saying, What mean ye by these stones?

We, like the people in the day of Joshua crossing the Jordan, can say this is what the Lord did. In the life of every church, God has performed some mighty works, from facilities being erected, addictions being broken, marriages being restored, drunks being saved, diseases being healed, etc. It is our responsibility to assure that God gets the glory and we not mishandle any blessing He has bestowed on the church. For God to bless the church, and the blessing not to be memorialized, is as sinful as Achan hiding God's accursed/devoted things in his tent under the ground.

> And Achan answered Joshua, and said, Indeed I have sinned against the LORD God of Israel, and thus and thus have I done: When I saw among the spoils a goodly Babylonish garment, and two hundred shekels of silver, and a wedge of gold of fifty shekels weight, then I coveted them, and took them; and, behold, they are hid in the earth in the midst of my tent, and the silver under it. (Joshua 7:20-21)

Achan was destroyed for his sin. We must destroy and burn our "Achans" so that God's house can be purified from the sin of stealing God's accursed/devoted glory. Memorializing God's good works in the life and history of the church to the glory of God will help this cause.

SOLUTION SEVEN: *Establish God-sized Tasks for the Church.*

The carnal side of believers tends to think that what they accomplish belongs to them. It is only when the task becomes impossible in their understanding do they tend to give God the glory. We owe it all to God, but man tends

When the task is a God-sized task from the beginning, we tend not only to rely on God, but attribute the credit to Him also.

to think that God only takes over when man has reached his limit. Such is sin. When the task is a God-sized task from the beginning, we tend not only to rely on God, but attribute the credit to Him also. God divinely knew this carnal (flesh) tendency in the days of Gideon when He reduced Gideon's army to such a small size that they would not be tempted to steal His accursed/devoted glory by claiming themselves as the victor.

And the Lord said unto Gideon, The people that are with thee are too many for me to give the Midianites into their hands, lest Israel vaunt themselves against me, saying, Mine own hand hath saved me. (Judges 7:2)

Churches must seize the opportunity to look for God-sized tasks to help deliver herself and break the stronghold of the sin of taking God's accursed/devoted things.

SOLUTION EIGHT: *Do Something Foolish for God.*

But God hath chosen the foolish things of the world to confound the wise; and God hath chosen the weak things of the world to confound the things which are mighty; And base things of the world, and things which are despised, hath God chosen, yea, and things which are not, to bring to nought things that are: That no flesh should glory in his presence. (1 Corinthians 1:27-29)

God tells us that He has chosen the foolish things of the world that no man should glory in His presence. Spiritually, there is a relationship between foolishness and faith; likewise there is a relationship between wisdom or reason and sight. To us, anything that cannot be reasoned is foolish, and that which can be reasoned or predicted is wise. God's word stands contrary to our wise and intellectual reasoning. For this reason, I believe that every once in a while we should do something foolish to demonstrate our faith in God. Although I am thankful for the intellectual skill God has given me, my fear of stealing His glory drives me to foolishly step out on faith.

By His Spirit God still commands the church to do foolish things in obedience to His will.

Think of the foolishness of marching around a city for seven days, and on the seventh day marching around seven times and shouting with a loud noise. But this was not such a foolish or silly march. This was a praise march of faith done in obedience to God's command.

By His Spirit God still commands the church to do foolish things in obedience to His will. God may ask the church to foolishly project a budget beyond its reason. God may ask a church to step out on faith in a mission field beyond its wildest thought. God may ask us to develop a praise team in the middle of a conservative tradition-al church worship setting. Yes, God might ask us to start a prayer march around the church in preparation for revival, or to run a victory lap around the sanctuary as many of us now do at the church I serve as pastor.

God wants to break our comfort zones of intellectual-ism for His glory. Doing something foolish for God con-tributes toward the killing of the sin of robbing God's glory by mishandling God's accursed/devoted things.

Skull Practice
CHAPTER NINE — MISHANDLING THE ACCURSED/DEVOTED THINGS OF GOD: STEALING GOD'S GLORY

1. What are the accursed/devoted things of God?
   They are the sacred things that are holy unto Him. They are the things that belong to Him alone, and are set aside for Him alone.

2. Why did God prohibit the Israelites from keeping any of the spoils of their victory over Jericho and other Canaanite cities?
   Because the spoils represented the evil practices and idolatry of the Canaanite people.

3. For what reason did God say that the Israelites lost the first battle at Ai?
   Because a member of the camp named Achan stole some of God's accursed/devoted things.

4. How does God want us to treat the sin of mishandling accursed/devoted things?
   He wants us to intentionally, intensely, and utterly destroy this sin.

5. According to the catechism, what is the chief aim of man?
   The chief aim of man is to glorify God and enjoy Him forever.

Fill in the Blanks

1. The tithe that is holy unto God can be considered as an
   _____ _____ _____. (accursed/devoted thing)

2. God's anointed church leaders can be considered as
   _____ _____ _____. (accursed/devoted things)

3. God's church, which He not only died for, but is coming back to claim, can be considered as an _____
   _____ _____. (accursed/devoted thing)

4. The Garden of Eden, specifically the tree of knowledge
   of good and evil, was an _____ _____ _____.
   (accursed/devoted thing)

5. God's glory is God's passionate _____ _____
   _____. (accursed/devoted thing)

Helpful Dialogue

1. This chapter introduces the term "clergy killers." Do they
   exist in your church? If clergy killers exist in your
   church, without identifying persons or naming names,
   discuss solutions. If clergy killers do not exist in your
   church, explain the blessing of why they are not present.

2. The law of Moses and the apostle Paul write, "thou
   shall not muzzle the ox that treadeth out the corn."
   Discuss interpretations of this scripture. Is the pastor of
   your church allowed to lead, or is your church gov-

erned by well meaning, or maybe not so well meaning, but definitely unscriptural boards? What would happen if an anointed, spirit-filled pastor was allowed to lead your church?

3. Churches today have been infected by the philosophy of humanism. What is this philosophy, and in what way is it manifested in the church? What are some solutions and remedies to cure it?

4. Worship is God's party. Yet, He allows us to party hearty (have fun and enjoy) His party. What is the relationship of this statement to our theology of glory and the chief aim of man according to the catechism?

5. Worship and work (service) both glorify God. Why, then, is it stated that prioritizing worship before service assures the continuation of His glorification.

What Will Happen If This Problem Is Not Resolved?

1. Personal, church, and community destruction of a sort will become apparent.

2. The church will exist under a curse.

3. A Christian blessing will be cut off or limited.

4. Prayer will be stifled.

5. Praise and worship will not be acceptable.

CHAPTER TEN

Christian Apathy

One of the greatest afflictions of the Christian church is apathy. Other words that describe apathy are indifference, dull, sleepy, unresponsive, and lethargic. Apathy comes from Greek words meaning "no feeling." Interestingly, the word anesthesia also comes from Greek words meaning "no feeling." Satan has masterfully taken on the role of an aesthetician, and has gradually put the church in a state of numbness. Some churches have overdosed and are literally in a coma. Others are more than comatose, they are indeed the walking dead among the living.

Jeff Treder writes:

In medical practice, an anesthetic is usually a carefully controlled dosage of a poison, an overdose of which will kill the patient. The enemy of our souls has managed to do the reverse of this to the church—and he has managed it because we have allowed it, given our consenting nod to the smiling anesthetician. With our consent, the enemy has been able to limit our dosage of the good things of the Spirit–limited doses of spiritual worship, knowledge of the Scriptures, koinonia fellowship, evangelistic outreach. Limited doses, just enough to lull us into a comfortable spiritual complacency. It turns out that limited doses of heavenly things can act as a soporific drug, an efficient anesthetic.[1]

Christian apathy could be the worst of sins because it is an anesthetic that covers up all our sin problems.

Christian apathy could be the worst of sins because it is an anesthetic that covers up all our sin problems. Apathy has caused the church to develop a "Who cares?" attitude. Who cares whether the "next" or "X" generation gets saved? Seemingly, nobody really cares. The church, obviously, does not care enough to change its methods of presenting the gospel. What a tragic state the church finds herself in! No one seems to care about what really matters most. We claim obedience to Christ by striving to have the mind of Christ.

For who hath known the mind of the Lord, that he may instruct him? But we have the mind of Christ. (1 Corinthians 2:16)

The mind of Christ is not apathetic. Suppose Jesus had been apathetic.

Ed Bousman illustrates.

"Lord do you want me to give ten percent or two percent? Suppose the Lord said, I don't care whether you give anything or not. Lord how many services do you want me to attend? Suppose the Lord said, I don't care whether you ever come or not. It is no concern of mine. If you would rather stay home and look at television that is fine with me. I could not care less. If you come or don't come I won't miss you either way. Suppose the Lord had that idea about your prayer life. I don't care whether you pray or not. The only time you pray anyway is when you want something. If you do pray I'll listen to you if I don't have anything better to do. Lord, do you mean to say that you don't really care if I miss the Lord's Supper and go to a ball game? Suppose the Lord said, do as you please. I don't care what you do. As to His coming again, suppose the Lord said, I may return and then again maybe I won't. We have too many things going on here in Heaven for Me to be concerned about coming back down there again. I simply don't care one way or the other about returning to your crummy world. Actually we can get along quite well here in Heaven without you. So what would we think if the Lord was as indifferent about us as we are about Him."[2]

Jesus was not apathetic so neither should His church be. If we are apathetic, we have not only missed the mark, we have missed the whole target. Apathy, therefore, is sin.

The apathetic person simply does not care. He has insulated himself from the pain in the world and often the pain within himself. Apathy is the worst of modern sins. It may be termed as "sloth." Slothfulness is not just laziness, it is apathy toward good. It is displaying a "Who cares?" attitude toward that which makes life worth living. It is indifference directed at who God created us to be. It is blatant rebellion against God's purpose. It is arrogant sin against the love of God. The opposite of apathy is empathy. Those who are not apathetic are usually empathetic. An empathetic person is responsive and feels very deeply. They also feel deep pity, sorrow, grief, and misery. An empathetic person has compassion. Compassion is to feel pain with someone else.

The prophet Nehemiah was such a person. Nehemiah was burdened for the Old Testament people of God. When he heard of their pitiful condition and distress, he sat down and wept.

> And they said unto me, The remnant that are left of the captivity there in the province are in great affliction and reproach: the wall of Jerusalem also is broken down, and the gates thereof are burned with fire. And it came to pass, when I heard these words, that I sat down and wept, and mourned certain days, and fasted, and prayed before the God of heaven. (Nehemiah 1:3-4)

If we examine the church today, we will find that the walls of compassion are broken down and the gates of burden for a lost and dying world are on fire. Like Nehemiah, the church needs to sit down and weep, pray, and fast over the apathy that plagues the church. Remember, Jesus wept over the sins of Jerusalem.

> And when he was come near, he beheld the city, and wept over it. (Luke 19:41)

Very important however, is that Nehemiah and Jesus moved beyond just being empathetic and having compas-

The Christian antidote for apathy is zeal, service, and a fiery spirit.

sion. They both had solutions. If compassionate people have no solutions, they are simply pathetic. People with solutions are usually zealous. The Christian antidote for apathy is zeal, service, and a fiery spirit:

Never be lacking in zeal, but keep your spiritual fervor, serving the Lord. (Romans 12:11, NIV)

It is not surprising that people often escape their empathetic state by becoming apathetic. They "grow weary in well doing" (Galatians 6:9; 2 Thessalonians 3:13). They just quit feeling and caring. Scripture says that the love of many will grow cold.

BIBLICAL EXAMPLES

Several examples of apathy are found in the Bible. In 1 Kings 18:21, Elijah confronted the fence straddlers of his day. The inspired prophet wrote:

How long halt ye between two opinions? if the Lord be God, follow him: but if Baal, then follow him. And the people answered him not a word.

The indifferent people of Elijah's day showed no interest or emotion to the challenge. The "who cares" attitude was very obvious. Amos provided another example of apathy when he announced woe upon the ruling aristocrats of Judah and Israel who were secure in their power and wealth. He wrote:

Woe to them that are at ease in Zion, and trust in the
mountain of Samaria, which are named chief of the
nations, to whom the house of Israel came. (Amos 6:1)

These people looked at their material wealth and the
defenses of their fortified mountain city and felt smug,
confident, and secure. Their arrogant, self-sufficient attitude resulted in an attitude of "who cares."

Perhaps the best example of apathy found in the
Bible is in the church at Laodicea. It represents a
sad picture of much of the professing churches in
the world throughout the history of the Christian
era, and illustrates those who participate in the
outer religious worship without the inner reality.[3]

The church at Laodicea was comfortable and complacent in self-satisfaction. Secure, like the people of
Amos' day, they can also be compared to those Elijah
addressed as they showed no emotion. Jesus addressed
their problem:

Because thou sayest, I am rich, and increased with
goods, and have need of nothing; and knowest not
that thou art wretched, and miserable, and poor,
and blind, and naked: I counsel thee to buy of me
gold tried in the fire, that thou mayest be rich; and
white raiment, that thou mayest be clothed, and
that the shame of thy nakedness do not appear; and
anoint thine eyes with eyesalve, that thou mayest
see. (Revelations 3:17- 18)

The problem of apathy has been identified as an attitude problem which surfaced in the Laodicean church in

the form of lukewarmness. They had no enthusiasm, no emotion, no zeal, no urgency. These people, neither cold nor hot, were somewhere in the middle.

> So then because thou are lukewarm, and neither cold nor hot, I will spew thee out of my mouth. (Revelation 3:16)

The sin of apathy, which is a lukewarm attitude, did not end with Laodicea; it is now present in the contemporary local church.

SIGNS OF APATHY

The signs of apathy are reflective of many other sins previously listed in this book, such as saint selfishness, unbiblical worship, cursed giving and others. This is why it is the worst of modern day sin. Signs of apathy can be seen in the following:

Lukewarm Preachers

Many churches know nothing but lukewarm preaching. If the Holy Ghost power returns to those in the pew, it must first return to those in the pulpit. Churches desperately need men in the pulpit who preach from the heart.

There is a scarcity of heart preaching today. Few preachers seem to have the element of "heart" in their preaching styles. Yet, a casual survey of the preachers in the Bible indi-

> Churches desperately need men in the pulpit who preach from the heart.

"When the leaders of the church, especially the male leaders of the church, begin to praise God according to His will, a transforming power will come over the church as never before."

cates that they preached not only from their heads but also from their hearts.[4]

Lukewarm Parishioners

It should also be pointed out that the preacher is not solely responsible for the lukewarmness in the church. In many churches there is fire in the pulpit but frost in the pews. A casual glance at the congregation on Sunday morning reveals that although there is a melt-down in the pulpit, there is a freeze-over in the pews.

The goal of many church goers is to become as comfortable as they can during the sermon. Sometimes this comfortable state leads them to become drowsy and some may even become comatose! Rather than being on the edge of their seat eager to hear, they reflect a "who cares" attitude. They are just like the Laodiceans. The reason this attitude exists in today's church is that people are self-satisfied and feel that they have no need for anything. They are self-sufficient.

Lukewarm Praises

The sin of apathy which is an attitude of lukewarmness is also evident in praise, or the lack thereof. Many churches need to rediscover the power of expressive praise and what praising God will do for the congregation.

> "When the leaders of the church, especially the male leaders of the church, begin to praise God according to His will, a transforming power will come over the church as never before."[5]

Every born-again child of God should discover ways to express themselves to God in praise. There are several ways to be expressive in praise such as kneeling, raising hands, clapping, crying, and vocal affirmations of the goodness of God. God desires for His children to express themselves to Him in praise. Further, God is deserving of the praise He desires.

Why, then, is there a lack of praise in so many congregations? The reasons are numerous, but it may be because many congregations have become so complacent that they have no desire to praise the Lord. There is a great need in many churches to reclaim this mighty power.

Lukewarm Giving

The problem of Christian apathy, which has been defined as an attitude of lukewarmness, is also reflected in the attitude of the membership concerning tithing. Many believers are lukewarm in their giving to God but are red hot in their giving to themselves. Many feel it is the responsibility of someone else to give the tithe. Many celebrate their increase in finances by buying something nice for themselves. Those same believers never consider giving an increase back to the one who gave it to them.

Being a follower of Christ means telling others about Him. The tragedy is that not many Christians are doing this.

Lukewarm Witnessing

Perhaps the greatest tragedy is luke-warm witnessing. The "Who cares?" attitude always results in no one sharing Christ. Being a follower of Christ means telling others about Him. The tragedy is that not many Christians are doing this. They are being hindered by a lukewarm attitude toward evangelism.

At its core, evangelism is making known the good news of Jesus Christ to a dying world.[6]

Evangelism is sharing the death, burial and resurrection of Jesus for the purpose of seeing others commit their lives to Him. Rather than share the gospel, many people simply make excuses. Some excuse themselves by passing on the responsibility to the pastors, deacons, and Sunday School teachers.

Others excuse themselves due to a lack of knowledge of scripture. Some say they don't witness because people cannot be won to the faith. Anybody can be won to Christ if you discover the key to his or her heart. It is very critical that the church overcome this lukewarm attitude toward witnessing.

The Source of Apathy

Where does this attitude of lukewarmness come from? What is the source of apathy? To answer these questions, one simply needs to look at Laodicea.

Because thou sayest, I am rich and increased with goods, and have need of nothing; and knowest not that thou art wretched, and miserable, and poor, and blind, and naked (Revelation 3:16-17). These sources seem apparent: an unfaithful heart, a false security, and a deceived mind.

An Unfaithful Heart

The root cause of this sad condition goes back to the first of the seven churches addressed by Christ. Laodicea, just like the church at Ephesus, had forsaken her first love. The source of apathy is an unfaithfulness to the Lord Jesus Christ. Any time a believer begins to love someone or something more than they love the Lord, chances are good that apathy will take over.

> **Any time a believer begins to love someone or something more than they love the Lord, chances are good that apathy will take over.**

A true indication of the Laodicean church's unfaithfulness is seen in the fact that she speaks of herself and not of Christ. She boasts of her material riches and resources but never says one word of praise about the Lord Jesus Christ. Ephesus and Laodicea are not the only churches that have left their first love. As a matter of fact, what was true of these churches is also true of many local churches today.

There are far too many believers who love money and the things it can buy more than they love God. Should the conclusion be drawn that to have things is wrong? Is it wrong to have material things? No, it only becomes displeasing to God when the believer loves things more than he or she loves God.

False Security

Another source of apathy is a false security. The Laodiceans felt secure because they were rich and had plenty. The bills were paid, the children were healthy, and the bank account was full. For the Laodiceans, the false security gave way to a "who cares" attitude. There was no need for God because they were financially blessed. "The church at Laodicea was not burdened with debt, but it was burdened with wealth."[7]

Jesus spoke a parable about another man who felt himself to be secure because of what he had. The parable is mentioned in Luke 12:13-21. According to Jesus, there was a man whose crops had been blessed greatly. His barns were full, and there was no room to put the crops that needed to be gathered. The man felt self-sufficient and therefore reasoned within himself. The decision was made to tear down the existing barns and build bigger ones. The future looked bright and secure, but something unexpected happened.

> Luke wrote, But God said unto him, Thou fool, this night thy soul shall be required of thee: then whose shall those things be, which thou hast provided? So is he that layeth up treasure for himself, and is not rich toward God. (Luke 12:20- 21)

The Laodiceans and the rich man serve as a warning to today's church as to where security is really found. No one should place their security in the world's riches. Christ is the only anchor that will hold.

A Deceived Mind

The final source of apathy to be mentioned is a deceived mind. It is evident from scripture that the Laodiceans had been deceived. They thought that because they were wealthy they had no need for anything else. The Laodiceans saw themselves as one thing, but Jesus Christ saw them as they really were. The revelation of Christ to them reveals just how deceived they were.

The sin of apathy is patient and insidious. It is found in those whose faith has become more habit than love; more ritualistic than committed; more duty than relationship.

The Laodiceans saw themselves as rich. But Jesus revealed they had been deceived. Although they were rich in the things of the world, they were poor when it came to spiritual matters. The Laodiceans were described by Christ as "blind," meaning they were unable to perceive spiritual things.

The modern church is just as deceived as the Laodiceans. The modern church sees only with the natural eye. The material things are what really matter and there is no regard to spiritual riches.

An unfaithful heart, a false security and a deceived mind will always lead to apathy. "Laodicea had been reduced to room temperature. It was neither hot nor cold, neither one thing or the other. It was marked by complete compromise."[8] This is the sad state of apathy.

Reasons for Apathy

The sin of apathy is patient and insidious. It is found in those whose faith has become more habit than love; more ritualistic than committed; more duty than relationship. "Apathy comes when a person seeks to conform outwardly to the way of Christ without ever having made a personal commitment. Without the decision to submit our hearts and lives to Him we are left trying to live a Christian lifestyle without his power. It simply cannot be done, human flesh does not have the capacity. It is possible to remain in this state of apathetic failure for years by force of habit. Perhaps you have visited a church like this. Do not be deceived into thinking this is Christianity."[9]

Peter Wilkes goes on in his book, *Defeating the Dragons of the Soul,* to elaborate on several reasons for apathy. They are:

The Fear of Being Different – Our society frowns on Christian enthusiasm. It is perfectly alright to be enthusiastic about other things like sports, our children, movies, the theater; but to be enthusiastic about Christianity is not a part of society's value system.

The Attraction of Sin – Sin makes apathy easy. Let us not fool ourselves, if sin were not alluring, we would not fall into it. Satan spends a lot of time making sin very attractive.

It is past time for the church to clean up its mess and awaken from its drugged stupor.

The Cost of Discipleship – The cost of discipleship is played down. Jesus' approach to discipleship does not fit very well with our modern, goal-oriented approaches. Salvation is free, but there is a cost for discipleship. Salvation called for a sacrifice from Jesus; discipleship calls for a sacrifice from us.

Cleaning Up the Pew

It is past time for the church to clean up its mess and awaken from its drugged stupor. Enthusiasm has cooled, the church has fallen asleep, and tares have been sown among the wheat. The house was made to be clean, but apathy has allowed it to become filthy.

Jesus said, it makes me sick!

I know thy works, that thou art neither cold nor hot: I would thou wert cold or hot. So then because thou art lukewarm, and neither cold nor hot, I will spew thee out of my mouth. (Revelations 3:15-16)

I believe that the church to whom these words were written is the collective church of today. It is the only church in the Book of Revelation that Jesus was totally disgusted with. The church did not even merit His respect. This is the only sin that made Jesus sick! Jesus has describes His feeling toward apathy as a regurgitation from the depths of the viscera. The grossness and intensity of the picture should drive us to a state of awakeness. The church should be on her knees in a posture of confession and repentance, literally wailing for forgiveness. Apathy is sin in the house.

Because of doctrinal disagreement and the many interpretations of the book of Revelation and eschatology, mainline churches have basically avoided teaching and preaching on the end times.

HOUSE CLEANING SOLUTIONS
SOLUTION ONE: *Teach and Preach Biblical Prophesy*

Because of doctrinal disagreement and the many interpretations of the book of Revelation and eschatology, mainline churches have basically avoided teaching and preaching on the end times. Others have had a field day with dogma claiming to know the absolute sequence of time and events relative to the coming of the end. Mainline churches have been satisfied with the spiritual truth spoken by Jesus, that we know not the day nor the hour (Matthew 24:36; Mark 13:32).

The total dependence on this truth has caused the church to become apathetic. Knowing the truths of prophecy ignite a much needed sense of urgency. Plus, the knowledge of prophecy is beneficial for daily living. Knowledge and understanding of what is coming better prepares and equips us for what is currently being encountered. There are blessings in understand-

Do not avoid teaching prophecy.

ing prophecy. Teach and emphasize prophecy, even if it means teaching all the various interpretations.

The heart of the prudent getteth knowledge; and the ear of the wise seeketh knowledge. (Proverb 18:15)

Do not avoid teaching prophecy. On the day of judgement, apathy will have no place. Teach and preach prophecy and develop a sense of urgency –

I must work the works of him that sent me, while it is day: the night cometh, when no man can work. (John 9:4)

SOLUTION *TWO: Emphasize Spiritual Warfare*

Many churches have underestimated the presence of Satan and evil in the world. Christians wake up every morning not aware of the presence of Satan and the weaknesses of their own flesh. The person of Satan is real. He is the prince of this world. If you do not understand his existence, every attack is an ambush.

The question may be asked, Have you met Satan today? The answer is, if you have not you both must be walking in the same direction. God calls us not to walk side by side with Satan.

We are to walk after the Spirit, and not after the flesh (Romans 8:1,4). Apathy has proven to be one of Satan's greatest weapons. It is like a gas that has caused the church to go to sleep at the gospel plow. The church is under attack. The church must fight back. God has warned us that,

> We wrestle not against flesh and blood, but against principalities, against powers, against the rulers of the darkness of this world, against spiritual wickedness in high places. (Ephesians 6:12)

Therefore, we must put on the whole armor of God and fight apathy daily.

SOLUTION THREE: *Expect All Church Auxiliaries to Participate in at Least One Mission Project and One Evangelistic Event per Year (especially the administrative auxiliaries such as trustee and finance committees)*

Jesus said that if we are to find ourselves, we must lose ourselves (Matthew 10:39;16:25). Therefore, a steady diet of missions and evangelism will help us find our way back from laziness and slothfulness.

People in decision making positions have generally been lured further than others and a double dose of missions and evangelism may be required for them. Remember, if the leadership is lost in the sin of apathy, the followship is farther lost. Serving God and doing His specific agenda is a powerful solution for apathy.

SOLUTION FOUR: *Promote a Balanced Christian Life*

An old adage states that all work and no play makes Jack a dull boy. Well, all seriousness and no fun makes Christians apathetic saints. Rest and relaxation (R&R) are necessary so that we don't grow weary in well doing.

Sometimes our pride keeps us working on projects that God has removed us from.

Christians who love the Lord can grow weary. Tiredness is a danger to the Christian worker. Weariness is a friend of the enemy. When we are weary, we are weak and vulnerable.

Where does weariness come from? First, weariness comes from doing too much. There are only twenty-four hours in a day. Although it does not take a rocket scientist to figure this out, many of us behave as if we have more than twenty-four. One of the most meaningful lessons God has taught me is that I do not have to do everything. All I need to do is be faithful over a few things.

Second, weariness comes from pride. It is a real ego problem to think that you are the only one who can accomplish a task. Sometimes our pride keeps us working on projects that God has removed us from. Christians must strive to live balanced lives. Christians need time for their families, their personal devotion, their leisure, their friends, their worship, as well as their work. Paul tells us:

> Let us not be weary in well doing: for in due season we shall reap, if we faint not. (Galatians 6:9)

SOLUTION FIVE: *Teach Commitment as a Core Value*

Example: Core Value #22 from the Greenforest Community Baptist Church. "We believe that a personal demonstrative commitment is a powerful Christian witness. This includes annually signing commitment cards

Apathy comes when one's faith is motivated from habit rather than from love. Apathy is defeated by love, and love is a choice.

concerning the giving of our time, gifts, talents and money." The fire of genuine Christianity is sparked by decision. You cannot become a Christian by osmosis. You must make a personal response.

Apathy is fueled by indecisiveness and lack of commitment. The church today tends to shy away from commitment. Apathy comes when one's faith is motivated from habit rather than from love. Apathy is defeated by love, and love is a choice.

Churches should encourage their members to make personal commitments to all the admonishments of God and expectations of the church. Not only in the area of money, but attendance, discipleship, worship, etc. Christians should be asked to commit to Christian behavior according to agreed upon interpretation of scripture. Apathy is destroyed by a definitive commitment to model Christ.

SOLUTION SIX: *Vary the Methods of Presenting the Gospel*

Variety has been said to be the spice of life. Today's church needs a good shot of spice to be delivered from the sin of apathy. Without question, there can be no change in the message–the Good News *(kerigma)* should never be compromised in even the slightest manner. The adage, "there is more than one way to skin a cat," is applicable to the gospel.

There is more than one way to bring the lost sinner to God. There is more than one way to call for a decision to Christian commitment. There is more than one way to teach the Bible. There is more than one way to preach the gospel. There is more than one way to worship God, and more than one manner of edification.

Many churches are locked into the tradition of doing everything, every year, the same way. Christians must learn to be products of tradition, but not victims of tradition.

Many churches are locked into the tradition of doing everything, every year, the same way. Christians must learn to be products of tradition, but not victims of tradition. Doing the same thing the same way over and over again causes the root of apathy to gain hold of our lives.

A cafeteria hot line or salad bar menu approach to presenting the most important things will help break the declining cycle that has produced this evil of sin in the house.

SOLUTION SEVEN: *Teach the Scriptural Prescription for Apathy*

Two specific prescription scriptures are Romans 12:11 and Revelation 3:17b-22. These prescriptions have been incorporated into, and undergird all the previously listed solutions. The *Weekly Sunday*

School Lesson Notes did an excellent exposition of these scriptures. The following are excerpts from these notes.

Romans 12:11: Never be lacking in zeal, but keep your spiritual fervor, serving the Lord. (NIV)

The Greek word for "zeal" can mean diligence or earnestness. It refers to something done eagerly, with great haste and great effort. It stands in direct opposition to a "who cares" attitude. "Be fervent in spirit." The Greek words imply an enthusiastic or devoted spirit. The word is used elsewhere in Acts 18:25 to describe Apollos, who was said to have a fervent spirit. A fervent spirit is a delightful rarity among Christians today.

When Paul says "Serve the Lord," literally, Paul says "be enslaved" to the Lord Jesus. The image is one of wholly putting aside one's own callings, desires, and expectations, and allowing the Lord Jesus to be the absolute master.

Revelation 3:17b-22: Knowest not that thou art wretched, and miserable, and poor, and blind, and naked: I counsel thee to buy of me gold tried in the fire, that thou mayest be rich; and white raiment, that thou mayest be clothed, and that the shame of thy nakedness do not appear; and anoint thine eyes with eyesalve, that thou mayest see. As many as I love, I rebuke and chasten: be zealous therefore, and repent. Behold, I stand at the door, and knock: if any man hear my voice, and open the door, I will come in to him, and will sup with him, and he with me. To him that overcometh will I grant to sit with me in my throne, even as I also overcame, and am set down with my Father in his throne. He that hath an ear, let him hear what the Spirit saith unto the churches.[10]

- **Remember what matters.** Jesus counsels the Laodiceans to buy from Him "gold refined by fire." The Laodiceans were well-known traders and merchants—yet Jesus reminds them that the riches which He offers are the ones which will make a difference. In the midst of everyday living, have we forgotten what's really of eternal significance?

- **Repent.** Jesus further instructs His people to buy from Him "white robes to clothe you." They were to re-don the white robes which originally represented their new cleanness before the Lord. Apathy is a sin—and we won't truly get over it unless we reach the definite turning point which only genuine repentance can provide.

- **Seek God's counsel.** Jesus tells the Laodiceans next to receive "salve to anoint your eyes so that you may see." It is my contention that a Christian who is daily seeking the truth from God's Word, and who is daily letting God speak to his or her heart regarding what he or she needs to be doing in this world, will be unable to become apathetic!

Skull Practice
CHAPTER TEN — CHRISTIAN APATHY

1. Define apathy.
   Apathy may be defined as indifferent, dull, sleepy, unresponsive, or lethargic.

2. What is meant by empathetic?
   Empathetic means to be responsive, feel pity, pain, and compassion.

3. Is empathy a cure for being apathetic?
   No! Certainly we should be empathetic and have compassion and feel the pain of others. But empathy without a solution can lead to more apathy.

4. What is the cure for apathy?
   The cure for apathy is zeal. A fervent (fiery) spirit to render service to the Lord (Romans 12:11).

5. Summarize the prescription given to the church at Laodicea for their sin of apathy manifested as luke-warmness.
   They were to: (1) remember what matters—"buy of Him gold refined by fire;" (2) repent—"buy of Him white robes to be clothed;" (3) seek God's counsel— "receive salve to anoint your eyes so you may see."

Fill in the Blanks

1. _____ comes from the Greek word meaning "no feeling." (Apathy)

2. _____ could be considered the worst sin of modern day because it covers up and hides our general sin problem. (Apathy)

3. If we have the mind of Christ, and model Christ, we will not be _____. (apathetic)

4. One result of the sin of _____ is a "who cares" attitude. (apathy)

5. An attitude of "who cares" about "what matters most" is a display of the sin of _____. (apathy)

Helpful Dialogue

1. Signs of apathy include: (1) lukewarm preachers; (2) lukewarm parishioners; (3) lukewarm praise; (4) lukewarm giving; and (5) lukewarm witnessing. Are any of these signs demonstrated in any church you know? What two signs have you seen most often in your familiar church settings.

2. Sources of apathy that seem apparent are an unfaithful heart, a false security, and a deceived mind. Discuss the ramifications and implications of these sources of apathy.

3. The sin of apathy, manifested as lukewarmness, is the only sin of the seven churches of Asia Minor that made

Jesus sick. Why was Jesus so disgusted with luke-warmness that He wanted to vomit.

4. It has been suggested that to teach a knowledge and understanding of biblical prophesy will help eliminate the problem of apathy. How so? What is the relationship between understanding prophesy and apathy?

5. It has been suggested that a steady diet of missions and evangelism will help us find our way back from laziness and slothfulness. How does scripture support this suggestion? Do people in the decision making positions participate in missions and evangelism? What would happen if all the presidents, chairmen, finance committee persons, board members, auxiliary/ministry leaders, coordinators, and directors would go door-to-door in your community evangelizing?

What Will Happen If the Problem Is Not Resolved?

1. Revival will remain a thing of the past.

2. Satan will take far too many people to hell with him.

3. Less and less of each generation will come to know Christ.

4. The church as we know it today will one day become extinct.

5. Our children will die and go to hell before many of us die and go to heaven.

Endnotes

CHAPTER SIX

¹Lynn Anderson, ed., *In Search of Wonder* (Louisiana: Howard Publishing Company, 1995), 8.

²William H. Gentz, *The Dictionary of Bible and Religion* (Nashville: Abingdon Press, 1986), 1122.

³Don McMinn, The Practice of Praise (USA: Word Music, 1992), 64.

⁴Joe R. Stacker, *Authentic Worship: Exalting God and Reaching People* (Nashville: Convention Press, 1990), 8.

⁵*Ibid*, 8.

CHAPTER SEVEN

¹C.A. Tindley, "Some Day"

CHAPTER EIGHT

¹Martin Luther King, Jr. "Letter from the Birmingham Jail," *Anti-Racism: Confronting the Sin,* by Elaine Jenkins, (General Board of Church and Society and the General Commission on Religion and Race of the United Methodist Church), 7.

²Jefferson D. Edmonds, Jr., *Purging Racism from Christianity* (Grand Rapids: Zondervan Publishing House, 1986), 23.

³*Ibid*, 116, 120.

⁴Jack R. Taylor, *The Hallelujah Factor* (Broadman Press: Nashville, 1983), 71.

CHAPTER NINE

[1]John Piper, *God's Passion for His Glory* (Wheaton, IL: Crossway Books, 1998), 36.

[2]*Ibid*, 32-33

CHAPTER TEN

[1]Jeff Treder, "Antidote for Apathy." (http://www.tele-var.com/–destiny/antidote.htm)

[2]Ed Bousman. "Apathy." (http://www.christianchurch-es.org/gifapa/ponder/p1997c.htm)

[3]John F. Walvoord, *The Revelation of Jesus Christ* (Chicago: Moody Press, 1966), 93.

[4]Jerry Vines, *A Guide to Effective Sermon Delivery* (Chicago: Moody Press, 1986), 147.

[5]George O. McCalep, Jr., *Faithful Over a Few Things: Seven Critical Church Growth Principles* (Lithonia, GA: Orman Press, 1996), 62.

[6]Anthony T. Evans, *What Matters Most* (Chicago: Moody Press, 1997), 278.

[7]Clarence Larkins, *The Book of Revelation* (Glenside, PA: Rev. Clarence Larkins Estate, 1919), 28.

[8]John Phillips, *Exploring Revelation Revised* (Chicago: Moody Press, 1974), 73.

[9]Peter Wilkes, "Defeating the Dragons of the Soul" (http:sbcc.sbc.org/book2spt13.html)

[10]*Life and Work*, "Apathy," June 21, 1998 (Nashville: LifeWay Christian Resources), 54.